① woronstore . co[...] [...]s)
↳ modal

✱ arn[...]
↳ cu[...]

✱ aneko[...]tique . com
↳ cute lace undies
+ swim !!

The Pocket Guide to
SCOTTISH WORDS

✱ boody . co . uk → "cheap"
                    basics

✱ azurabay . com
↳ pretty undies not too
  exp. (some organic)
  WELCOME20 (20%) +tights
                    -swim

✱ pelechecoco . com
↳ leather, affordable

① WW RW → body, bras, swim

✱ Do you Green → competitive priced
bras

The Pocket Guide to
SCOTTISH WORDS

Iseabail Macleod

Richard Drew Ltd
Glasgow

Published by
Richard Drew Ltd
Redyett
Balfron
Glasgow G63 0RP

First published in 1986
Fully revised and updated 2006
reprinted 2017

A catalogue record for this book is
available from the British Library.

ISBN : 978-0-9552599-0-6

Typeset in ITC Garamond Condensed
Layout: Mark Blackadder

Printed and bound in China

CONTENTS

ACKNOWLEDGEMENTS

We are very grateful to the following for helpful advice and comment:

Scots-English	Pauline Cairns
Gaelic-English	Dr Donald William Stewart
Place-names	Ian Fraser, Dr Simon Taylor
Food	Catherine Brown
Beer	Stephen Sharp

INTRODUCTION

The purpose of this little book is to help tourists and newcomers to Scotland to understand some of the unfamiliar words, phrases and names they may meet. It includes Scots words, Gaelic words, place-name elements, personal names and some Scottish food and drink terms.

In a book of this size it is not possible to give more than a very brief introduction to all these subjects, but for those who would like to know more, there is list of books, websites and CDs on pp. 92-6.

Many people find the language situation in Scotland confusing. What is the Scots language? Who speaks Gaelic? Briefly, Scotland at the present time has three main languages:

English, the international language now the medium of administration and most formal writing and speech.

Scots, descended from a northern variety of Old English, which reached south-east Scotland in the 7th century. During the medieval period, it diverged from the more southerly dialects which eventually became standard English, but from the 16th century political events have drawn it closer to English. Today it is a continuum from Scottish Standard English, which differs more from its southern neighbour than most of its speakers realise, to demotic urban speech and rural dialects of considerable diversity.

Gaelic, the Celtic language of the Highlands and Islands, closely related to Irish. Over the centuries it has been pushed further and further to the northwest and the Western Isles, but it is now enjoying a revival with more support from the public and from government, especially in education, perhaps too little too late.

Other languages have a role with communities of

immigrants, such as Polish in the considerable numbers of Poles who remained in Scotland after World War II, and Asian languages in the different groups of more recent immigrants, including Chinese, Arabic, Urdu, Punjabi and Bengali.

Note that words in bold type in definitions are explained elsewhere in the book. See **elder** in Scots-English sections; **kirk session** is explained under **kirk**.

NB When looking up a **place-name**, look up its component parts. As well as the place-name section itself, try the Gaelic and Scots sections where words and spellings still in common use are to be found.

Notes on pronunciation

The pronunciation key set out below, with no special symbols except ə (the vowel in 'the'), can be used to reach *something like* the sounds of either Scots or Gaelic. This does not mean that Scots and Gaelic have the same sounds, nor yet that either has the same sounds as those represented by the same letters in Southern English. Far from it, but if you use the key carefully, you will at least be able to understand and to be understood.

It should be remembered that the pronunciation of both languages varies from area to area and in a book of this kind there is only room for one variety.

The following is a list of the letters used; note that : indicates a long vowel and that stressed syllables are printed in bold type.

Vowels

ə	as in	the, father
a	as in	pat
a:	as in	father
ay	as in	pay
e	as in	fed
ee	as in	week
Y	as in	bite
aee	as in	by
i	as in	sit
o	as in	lot
u	as in	hut
oa	as in	throat
oo	as in	school
aw	as in	bawl
ow	as in	fowl
aoo	approximately the same sound as *ow* above, but longer	
oy	as in	boy
oe	approximately as in French *oeufs* or German *Goethe*	

Consonants

Most consonants used in the key have *roughly* the same sounds as they have in English, but note: s as in see and g as in get.

    in Scots and Gaelic:

        ch   as in German *Bach* and *ich*

in Gaelic only:

        gh   pronounced similarly to ch, but voiced (ie using the vocal chords)

        ^y   a very slight y sound, as in English yes, at the end of a word

b, d, g   are sometimes given as p, t, k, but the actual sound is somewhere between the sounds of these letters in English.

There are three ways of pronouncing l in Gaelic, and many other points could be made. There is no space here, but if you would like to know more, see the list of books, websites and CDs on pp.92-6.

SCOTS – ENGLISH

Many people regard Scots as simply some kind of quaint
dialect made up of words like *hoots mon* (which few Scots
have ever heard off the English music hall stage), or simply
as bad English. In spite of its struggle against the supremacy
of English, Scots survives vigorously in the 21st century, and
contains words and phrases at all levels, including even
formal language, as well as words which all Scots use,
sometimes without even realizing they are Scottish.

One interesting category is legal language, the Scottish
legal system being quite different from the English. Like
education and the church, it was one aspect of Scottish life
which remained distinct from England after the Union of the
Parliaments in 1707. A few of the commoner legal terms
are included in this brief list.

Words and spellings which are limited to a particular
region have been marked (*North-East*), (*West*) etc.

a' [aw, a] all. **a'bodic** everybody.
abune [ə'bin] above.
academy name given to many Scottish secondary schools,
    eg *Leith Academy*.
ach expression of disgust, contempt etc.
advocate in the Scots legal system, the equivalent of a
    barrister; in Aberdeen, a solicitor.
ae [ay] one; a.
aff off.
agley [ə'glY] off the straight; wrong.
ahint behind.
aiblins perhaps.
ain own.
aince once.
aipple an apple.

airt a compass point; a direction.

alane alone.

ane, (*mainly East*) **yin**, (*mainly West*) **wan**, (*North-East*) **een** one.

anent about, concerning.

arbiter (*law*) an arbitrator.

ashet a (large) oval serving dish; (*West*) a pie dish.

astragal a window bar.

aucht eight; eighth.

auld old. **Auld Lang Syne** long ago.

ava at all.

avizandum *in Scots law*: (**ad**) **avizandum** for further consideration.

awa away, gone, left.

awfy awful.

aye[1] yes.

aye[2] always.

ayont beyond

bachle, bauchle [bachəl, bawchəl] (1) an old worn shoe or slipper. (2) a (small) clumsy, worn-out, untidy-looking person : *a wee bachle*.

back: at the back of five just after five. **the back end** late autumn.

bahookie (*informal*) the backside.

baith both.

bairn (*mainly East*) a child.

balmoral a kind of flat cap with a pompon on top and two ribbons behind, usually worn with Highland dress.

bampot, bammer a fool, idiot.

bap a kind of soft bread roll.

baronial of a style of architecture with crow-step gables, many small turrets etc, often seen on 19th-century mansions.

barrie (*South-East*) excellent, very good.

bauchle see **bachle**.

bawbee a halfpenny. **bawbees** money.

beadle a **church officer**.

beast a creature of any kind, a farm animal.

beds hopscotch.

ben[1] a mountain.

ben[2] : **ben** (**the hoose**) in or to another room of a house, sometimes the best room.

besom [bizəm] an unpleasant woman or girl.

bide to stay, live; to tolerate. **bidie-in** (*originally North-East*) an unmarried live-in partner.

bield protection; (a place of) shelter.

big to build. **biggin** a building.

bing a slag heap.

birk a birch tree.

birl to turn or whirl round rapidly.

blaeberry the bilberry, a small blue fruit found on moorland.

blate shy, timid, backward.

blether *verb* to talk too much (about nothing or about something untrue). *noun* a person who does this; a talk, chat. **blethers** foolish talk, nonsense.

blooter to strike hard; to kick (a football) with great force. **blootered** very drunk.

boak *verb* to vomit; retch, belch. *noun* a retch, belch; a feeling of sickness or disgust.

boggin smelly; very dirty; disgusting.

bogle a ghost, bugbear.

boiling a boiled sweet.

bonny lovely, pretty; handsome. **a bonny penny** a large amount of money.

bothy (1) a rough hut used by shepherds, fishermen, urban workers, mountaineers etc. (2) accommodation for unmarried male farmworkers. **bothy ballad** a song (as) sung by such farmworkers.

bowfin smelly; foul-tasting; very dirty; very bad, horrible.

brae a steep slope; a bank (of a river etc); a hillside.

braid broad.

bramble the blackberry (*fruit as well as bush*).

braw excellent, fine; handsome, fine-looking.

bree juice, liquid, especially that in which something has been cooked or soaked. **barley bree** whisky.

breeks trousers.

breenge to rush forward recklessly.

breid bread; (*North-East*) oatcakes.

bricht bright.

bridie, *also* **Forfar bridie** a kind of meat turnover.

brig a bridge.

brither a brother.

broch a circular prehistoric stone fort.

broth a thick meat and vegetable soup (see also **Scots**).

bubble *verb* to weep, cry. *noun* a fit of weeping. **bubbly jock** a turkey cock.

bucket a rubbish bin.

bum *verb* to boast. *noun* a boaster.

bunnet a soft flat peaked cap.

burgh (*till 1975*) a borough, a town with a corporation.

burn a stream, small river.

Burns Supper a celebration of the birthday of Robert Burns, usually a dinner with speeches and songs.

buroo unemployment benefit (office): *on the buroo*.

but and ben a two-roomed cottage.

butterie name used in other parts of Scotland for the North-East **rowie**.

ca [kaw, ka] to call; to drive; to set in motion (eg a skipping rope).

caber a large pole, tossed as a sport in Highland Games.

cairn a heap of stones, used eg as a marker or as a memorial.

cairry-oot food or drink bought for consumption elsewhere.

canny cautious; sparing; gentle, quiet. **no canny** unnatural.

capercailzie, capercaillie [kappər**kay**li] a very large bird of the grouse family, the wood grouse.

carfuffle a fuss, muddle, confusion.

carl a man.

carline an old woman.

carnaptious bad-tempered.

cauld cold.

causey a roadway, pavement, especially if cobbled.

ceilidh see Gaelic section.

champit mashed.

chanter the melody pipe of the bagpipe; a separate pipe for practising.

chanty a chamberpot.

chap *verb* to knock, strike; in dominoes etc, to knock on the table to indicate you can't play. *noun* a knock, blow; the stroke of a clock, bell. **chappit** mashed.

chaumer a room, chamber.

chiel(d) a young man; a child.

Church of Scotland the established Presbyterian church in Scotland, also known as **the Kirk**. **church officer** a person who is employed to carry out certain duties in a church, a sexton.

claes clothes.

clamjamfry, clanjamfry a crowd, rabble.

clan a family group, especially one originating in the Highlands or Borders.

clap to pat, stroke (eg an animal).

clarsach the small Highland harp.

clarty dirty, sticky.

claymore *originally* a large two-handed sword used by Highlanders in the Middle Ages; *later* also used to refer to a basket-hilted broadsword.

cleg a horsefly.

clishmaclaver gossip, chatter.

cloot a piece of cloth. **cloots** clothing. **clootie dumpling**
  a **dumpling** boiled in a cloth.
close (1) the passageway entrance into a **tenement**.
  (2) (*East*) a narrow passageway, especially a covered
  one between buildings.
clype *noun* a teller of tales. *verb* to tell tales.
cock-a-leekie chicken and leek soup.
college: the college the university.
Common Riding the **Riding of the Marches** in certain
  towns.
cone an ice-cream cornet.
convener a president, chairman.
coo a cow.
cookie a kind of plain round bun (see food section).
coorie to stoop, bend, crouch down.
coorse coarse, vulgar; wicked, bad; rough, awkward;
  (of weather) foul, stormy.
Corbett a mountain in Scotland of between 2500 and 3000
  feet (761 and 914 metres).
corbie the raven; the crow; the rook.
corn in Scotland usually refers to oats.
corrie see place-name section.
coup [cowp] *noun* an overturning, a fall; a rubbish tip.
  verb to overturn; to capsize; to empty by upturning.
couthie pleasant; friendly; comfortable, neat.
Covenanter a supporter of the Presbyterian church in the
  17th century.
crabbit bad-tempered.
craitur a creature, often used as a term of pity or contempt
  for a person.
craw a crow.
creel a large basket for carrying peat, fish etc.
creesh grease, fat.
croft a smallholding, especially in the Highlands. **crofter** a
  holder of such.

crowdie (1) (*in the Highlands*) a kind of rather crumbly soft cheese. (2) (*in the North-East*) a mixture of oatmeal and water.

cruik [kr(y)ook] a crook; a hook.

cry to call, give a name to. **cry-in** a visit

cuddy a horse; a donkey.

culpable homicide in Scots law, manslaughter.

cundy a street gutter; the grating over it.

dae to do.

daith death.

deacon the president of one of the **Incorporated Trades** of a town. **Deacon Converter** the **deacon** who presides over the **Incorporated Trades** of a town.

deave to deafen; to bore, irritate with constant talk etc.

dee to die.

deer forest a large tract of (now usually treeless) land, originally reserved for deer-hunting.

defamation in Scots law, = libel and slander.

defender in Scots law, a defendant (now only in civil cases).

deid dead.

deif deaf.

deil devil.

deochandorous [dyochəndorəs] a drink as one leaves.

depute deputy (*usually after the noun*): *convener depute.*

dicht *verb* to give a wipe or rub to, clean perfunctorily. *noun* a (quick) wipe, rub or wash.

ding to beat, strike. **go one's dinger** to do something or to act very vigorously.

dinna, dinnae do not.

dirk a short dagger, especially that worn in the belt as part of the Highland dress.

dirl *verb* to (cause to) tingle, vibrate, ring. *noun* something which causes such; the sensation thus produced.

dispone *in Scots law*, to convey (land).

divot a piece of turf, a sod.

dochter a daughter.

docken the dock plant.

dominie a schoolmaster.

Donald a hill in the Lowlands of 2000 feet (610 metres) or over.

doo a pigeon, dove. **doocot** [**doo**kət] a dovecote.

dook *verb* to duck; to bathe. *noun* a duck(ing); a bathe; a soaking. **dookin for aipples** the **Halloween** custom of trying to get hold of apples floating in a tub or basin with the teeth.

doon down. **doon the watter** down the river, used of the holiday resorts on the Clyde, popular in the early part of the 20th century.

doot to doubt; to suspect; to expect, rather think. *Also as noun:* **I hae ma doots**.

Doric the Scots language, now usually refers to North-East Scots.

douce [doos] quiet, pleasant, respectable, neat, tidy.

dour [door] stern, severe, stubborn; dull, humourless.

dram a drink of whisky (of whatever size).

drap drop.

dreep to drip; to descend from a wall etc by letting oneself down to the full stretch of the arms and dropping.

dreich [dreech] dreary, bleak, miserable (*often of weather*), dull, boring.

dripping roast something which is a constant source of profit.

drone a bass or tenor pipe of the bagpipe.

dross coal dust.

droukit [**droo**kit] drenched, soaked.

drouth [drooth] thirst; a drunk, a heavy drinker. **drouthy** thirsty; overfond of drink.

drove road a track formerly used by drovers taking animals, especially cattle, to and from market.

drystane dyke a stone wall without mortar.

dub a pool, pond, especially a muddy one.

dumpling a spicy fruit pudding, see **clootie dumpling**.

dunt (to give) a heavy blow (to).

dux the pupil who comes top in a school or class.

dwam a daydream, trance; a faint.

dyke a wall, especially of stone.

ee, *plural* **een** the eye.

een see **ane.**

efter after.

eident diligent, industrious.

elder a member of the governing body of a Presbyterian church, a member of the **Kirk Session**.

eneuch [inyooch] enough.

entry a passageway between buildings; an entrance to a building, especially to a block of flats.

erse arse.

ettle to intend, aim, attempt.

even on continuously.

fa[1] to fall.

fa[2] see **wha**.

factor an estate manager, land agent.

fae, **frae** from.

fair complete(ly), very.

Fair: the (Glasgow) Fair the traditional Glasgow summer holiday in the last two weeks of July; the first weekend of this period, the Monday being observed as a public holiday; also in other towns (especially in the West), in different fortnights. Compare **trades (holiday)**.

faither a father.

fan see **whan.**

fank a sheepfold.

fankle *verb, noun* tangle: **in a fankle**.

far: I could see him far enough I wish he were not
    here.

far see **whar.**

farl a three-cornered piece of oatcake, scone etc, a
    quartering of a round.

fash to annoy. **Dinna fash yersel.**

faur far.

fause false.

faut a fault.

feart afraid. **feartie** a coward.

feel (*North-East*) a fool.

fecht fight.

fegs exclamation of surprise or emphasis.

ferlie a marvel, wonder, object of curiosity.

feu until recently, a form of landholding by which land held
    in perpetuity from a superior under certain conditions;
    the most important of these was payment of a **feu duty.**

file (*North-East*) a while.

Finnan haddie a kind of smoked haddock.

fire-raising in Scots law, arson.

first: Tuesday first next Tuesday (*compare* **next**).

first-foot to be the first to visit a house in the New Year;
    this person is called a **first-foot** or **first-footer. to go
    first-footing** to visit friends early in the New Year,
    especially in its first few hours.

firth an estuary; a wide arm of the sea.

fiscal see **procurator fiscal.**

fit[1] see **whit.**

fit[2] a foot. **fitba** football.

fite (*North-East*) white.

flair a floor.

flesher a butcher.

flit to remove, move house. **flitting** a house removal.

foo (*North-East*) how.

foonds foundations.

footer *verb* to mess about, fiddle, act or work aimlessly.
noun a person who does this; an exasperating person; something awkward, more trouble than it is worth.

forby as well, in addition.

fore: to the fore still around, alive, in existence.

forenoon the morning.

forest see **deer forest**.

forfochen exhausted.

forkietail an earwig.

forrit forward.

fou full; drunk: **fou as a puggie** very drunk.

foust [foost] mould, mildew; a mouldy smell or appearance. **foustie** mouldy, musty, mildewy.

fower four.

fowk folk, people.

frae see **fae**.

Free Church originally, the church which broke away from the **Church of Scotland** in1843; now, the minority of it which refused to unite with the United Presbyterian Church in 1900, often known colloquially as the **Wee Frees**.

furth forth; outside, beyond the boundaries or confines of: **furth of Scotland**.

fushionless without energy, strength, ability, spirit or enthusiasm; insipid, dull.

fussle (*North-East*) whistle.

fykie fussy, finicky; tricky, awkward to do.

gadgie (*South-East*) a man, fellow.

gae to go. **gan, gaun** go(ing). **gaun yersel!** Expression of encouragement or appproval.

gallus (1) bold, cheeky, tough, wild. (2) (*West*) excellent, very good. **galluses** trouser braces.

gan see **gae**.

gang, (*North-East*) **ging** to go.

gar to make, cause to (see **grue**).

gas: put someone's gas at a peep to put someone in their place.

gaun see **gae**.

gean a wild cherry.

General Assembly the highest court of the **Church of Scotland** and other Presbyterian churches.

gey very.

gie to give.

gigot a leg of lamb or mutton.

gillie someone who attends on a sportsman shooting or fishing on a Highland estate.

gin if (only).

ging see **gang.**

ginger (*West*) a fizzy soft drink of any flavour.

girdle a flat iron plate with a handle, for baking over an open fire or other direct heat.

girn to moan, complain, grumble.

glabber soft wet mud.

glaikit (very) stupid, foolish.

glaur soft sticky mud.

gleg smart, quick(-witted).

glen a (narrow) valley.

glengarry a kind of forage cap, usually with two ribbons at the back.

gloaming twilight, usually the evening twilight.

goldie: wee goldie a drink of whisky.

gowan a daisy.

gowd gold.

gowf golf.

gowk a cuckoo; a fool (see **huntegowk**).

graip a garden fork.

graith equipment, gear

gralloch to remove the entrails of (a deer).

grannie a chimney cowl. **yer grannie** an expression of contempt or disbelief. *I think it's a comet. Comet yer grannie.*

green a piece of grassy ground around a house etc: **the back green**.

greet to cry, weep. **greetin teenie** a person who is always crying, moaning or complaining.

grieve an overseer of farmworkers.

grilse a young salmon which has only been to the sea once.

groset a gooseberry

grue *noun* a feeling of utter horror. *verb* to feel utter horror or fear. **It gars me grue**.

guddle to catch (fish) with the hands under the stones of a river etc; to mess about. *noun* a mess, muddle. **in a guddle**.

guff (to give off) a strong unpleasant smell.

guid, (*North-East*) **gweed** good.

guising: go guising (of children) to go round doors at Halloween offering to sing, recite etc in return for small gifts (especially apples or nuts) or money. **guiser** a child who does this; (*Shetland*) a member of one of the squads in the **Up-Helly-Aa** festival.

gushet a gusset; a corner, a triangular piece of land.

gweed see **guid.**

gyte mad, crazy.

haar a cold east-coast sea fog.

hackit ugly, unattractive.

haddie a haddock.

hae to have.

haggis a dish made of chopped offal, onions, spices etc, traditionally boiled in a sheep's stomach.

hail whole; undamaged.

hairst harvest.

haiver to talk nonsense. *Also as noun* **haivers**.

hame home.

handsel *noun* a gift to wish luck for something new. *verb* to celebrate (something new) (with such a gift).

hap cover, wrap.

harl (to) roughcast.

haud to hold.

hauf half.

haugh a river meadow.

heid the head. **heidbanger** a very stupid, crazy person. **heid bummer** a boss, the most important person in an organization. **heidie** a head teacher; (*in ball games*) a header. **high heid yins** those in authority.

hen term of endearment to a girl or woman. **hen-toed** pigeon-toed.

hert the heart.

het[1] hot.

het[2] (*in children's games*) it. *You're het.*

heugh [hyooch] a steep cliff; a deep gorge or ravine.

High Court (**of Justiciary**) the highest criminal court in Scotland.

Highers secondary school examinations at the more advanced level; a certificate for such.

hing to hang.

hirple limp, hobble.

hoast (to) cough.

Hogmanay New Year's Eve.

hoo how; why.

hoodie (**craw**) the hooded crow; the carrion crow.

hoolet, houlet an owl.

howe a hollow, low-lying ground.

howf a favourite place, eg a public house; a rough shelter.

howk to dig (up).

hunkers: on one's hunkers squatting.

huntegowk an April Fool; April Fools' Day; an April Fool's errand

hurdies the buttocks, hips.

hurl *noun* a ride or lift in a wheeled vehicle. *verb* to move, push, pull, in a wheeled vehicle.

ilk: that ilk the same place. **Moncreiffe of that ilk** = Moncreiffe of Moncreiffe; now also means kind, quality.

ilk(a) each, every. **of that ilk** (*in titles*) of that place.

Immortal Memory speech in honour of Robert Burns at a **Burns Supper**.

interdict a court order prohibiting something until the matter can be tried by court; compare English *injunction*.

ither other.

jag a prickle; an injection, an inoculation. **jaggie** prickly.

jalouse [jəlooz] to suspect, guess.

janitor, (*informal*) **jannie** a caretaker, especially in a school.

jeelie jelly; jam.

Jessie an effeminate man.

Jimmie familiar form of address to a man, especially a stranger.

joiner a carpenter, worker in wood.

jouk to dodge, avoid.

justiciary see **High Court**.

kail a kind of cabbage, especially a curly-leaved variety. **kailyard** literally a cabbage garden; used to describe a sentimental type of Scottish fiction popular in the late 19th and early 20th centuries.

keek peep.

keelie contemptuous term for a rough, tough man, especially a Glaswegian.

Kelvinside an over-refined, rather anglicized way of speaking (referring to a district of Glasgow).

ken to know.

kenspeckle easily noticed or recognised, conspicuous.

kilt a kind of knee-length skirt with pleats at the back, usually made of **tartan** and worn by men.

kirk a church. **the Kirk** the **Church of Scotland**. **kirk session** the lowest church court, administering the affairs of a congregation. **come into the body of the kirk** to come closer into a room, group of people etc.

kist a chest, box, trunk; a coffin.

knowe a knoll, little hill.

kye cattle.

lad(die) a boy, youth, young man; a son; a boyfriend. **lad o pairts** a young man of great promise.

laich, laigh [laych] low.

laird a landowner, landlord.

laldie a beating. **gie it laldie** to do something with a great deal of vigour.

Lallans the Scots language, especially a literary variety used by writers since the mid 20th century.

lang long.

lass(ie) a girl, young woman; a daughter; a girlfriend.

lat to let.

laverock the skylark.

law[1] a hill.

law[2] low.

leal loyal, faithful. **the land o the leal** heaven.

lee lie.

leet a list of candidates for a job: **long leet, short leet**.

leid a language.

licht light.

lift[1] *verb* to collect, gather; to harvest (e.g. potatoes); (*of the police*) to arrest.

lift[2] *noun* the sky.

line an authorization, eg an account with a shop, a note from a doctor stating incapacity for work, a prescription.

links[1] a stretch of usually grassy ground, often sandy, near the seashore; a golf-course (originally one on such ground); now mainly in place-names.

links[2] a string of sausages etc: *a pun o links.*

lintie a linnet.

loch a lake; an arm of the sea.

loon(ie) (*mainly North-East*) a boy, lad, youth; a son.

Lord Advocate the chief law officer of the Crown in Scotland. **Lord High Commissioner** the representative of the monarch at the **General Assembly** of the **Church of Scotland.** (See also **Lyon**.)

lowp leap, jump.

lowse to (become) loose, free

luckenbooth brooch a kind of heart-shaped silver brooch, formerly used as a love token or betrothal brooch; in former times, the **luckenbooths** were lockable stalls in the streets of Scottish towns.

lug an ear.

lum a chimney. **lum-hat** a top-hat.

Lyon: Lord Lyon the chief herald in Scotland and head of the **Lyon Court**.

mac familiar form of address to a man, especially a stranger.

Mackay [məkaee] **the real Mackay** the real thing.

maindoor flat a ground-floor flat with a door directly to the outside.

mair more.

maist most.

maister a master; a schoolmaster; (*as title*) Mr.

mak to make. **makar** a poet, especially a medieval one.

man a husband; also **mon, min** a way of addressing a person, especially to express surprise, exasperation etc.

manse the house provided for a Presbyterian minister. **son** or **daughter of the manse** the son or daughter of a minister.

march a boundary.

mask to infuse (tea).

maun must.

mavis a thrush.

meal *often refers specifically to* oatmeal.

meat food in general (as well as flesh).

meikle see **muckle**.

mercat a market.

merle *in poetry* a blackbird.

Merry Dancers the northern lights, aurora borealis.

messages shopping, things bought. **go the messages** to do the shopping.

micht might.

midden a dung heap; a rubbish heap; a rubbish bin.

mill lade a channel of water to a mill.

mind to remember; to remind.

mingin stinking; disgusting; very drunk.

minister a clergyman in one of the Presbyterian churches.

miss: miss oneself to miss something good by not being there.

mither a mother.

monie many.

morn morning. **the morn's morn** tomorrow morning.

morning roll a soft bread roll.

Morningside an over-refined, rather anglicized way of speaking (referring to a district of Edinburgh).

moolie mouldy; decayed, worn; stingy, mean.

moss (a stretch of) moorland or boggy ground.

mou [moo] a mouth.

muckle, meikle big.

muir a moor.

Munro a mountain in Scotland of 3000 feet (914.4 metres) or over. **Munro-bagging** the practice of climbing these, often aiming to climb them all. **Munro-bagger** a person who does this.

na, nae not. **nae weel** ill.

nane none.

neb a nose; a bird's beak; a tip or point.

neep a turnip.

Neerday [nayrday] New Year('s Day); a gift or hospitality given at this time.

neuk [nyook] a nook; a corner; a point of land.

next: Tuesday next the next Tuesday but one (*compare* **first**).

nicht night.

Nick: Auld Nick name for the Devil.

nieve a fist.

nip to tingle, smart, sting.

no not: **no bad** very good.

nocht nought, nothing.

noo now. **the noo** just now.

nor than.

numptie an idiot, stupid person.

nyaff term of contempt for a small, insignificant or nasty person.

o of.

och exclamation of sorrow, pain or annoyance.

ocht any(thing).

onie any.

oo wool.

oor[1] our.

oor[2] an hour.

oose fluff.

or before.

orra odd, spare, occasional. **orraman** odd-job man.

outwith outside, beyond.

ower over.

oxter an armpit.

Paddy's market a very untidy place (from the Glasgow street-market).

pan bread bread baked in a pan or tin. Also **pan loaf.**
   talk pan loaf speak in an affected, over-anglicized
   way.

panel the prisoner at the bar.

pape derogatory name for a Roman Catholic.

park an enclosed piece of farm land, a field, a football
   pitch. **parkie** child's word for a park attendant.

parritch porridge. **back tae auld claes an parritch**
   back to one's normal routine.

partan a crab. **partan bree** crab soup.

past: put past to put away for later use.

pauchle, pochle to cheat; to rig; to steal.

pawkie sly, cunning; humorous in a quiet, shrewd, dry-
   witted way.

pech to pant, puff, breathe hard.

peedie (*Orkney, Caithness, Fife*) small.

peel¹ a pill.

peel² a fortified house, a small defensive tower.

peelie-wally pale and ill-looking.

peer see **puir.**

peerie¹ (*Shetland, Orkney*) small.

peerie² a spinning top. **peerie heel** a stiletto heel.

peever(s) hopscotch.

pend an arched passageway, especially into the back court
   of a building.

perjink neat, tidy, prim; fussy, over-exact.

pey pay.

pibroch the classical music of the Scottish bagpipe; a piece
   of this with a theme and variations.

pickle, puckle a grain; a small particle or amount.

piece a piece of bread with butter, jam etc: *a jeelie piece.*

pig earthenware; an earthenware container, especially a
   hot-water bottle.

pinkie the little finger.

pirn a bobbin, spool.

pish piss.

piskie familiar name for an Episcopalian.

pit to put.

plain bread bread baked in batches of **plain loaves**,
which thus have a hard crust top and bottom and soft
sides.

pled past tense of plead.

plook a pimple, boil.

plowter to mess about in water; to potter about idly.

plunk to play truant from (school).

pochle see **pauchle**.

poind [pind] *in Scots law*, to seize and sell the goods
of a debtor.

poke a paper bag. **poly poke** a polythene bag.

policies the grounds round a large house.

pooch a pocket; a pouch.

pou to pull.

presbytery a church court above the **kirk session**.

press a large cupboard set into a wall.

procurator fiscal the public prosecutor in a **sheriff
court**; he also carries out some of the duties of an
English coroner.

Prod(die) derogatory name for a Protestant.

provost the equivalent of English mayor; since 1975
used only as courtesy title by some local authorities,
especially as **Lord Provost** in Edinburgh,
Glasgow, Aberdeen and Dundee; in the Scottish
Episcopal Church, the clergyman in charge of a
cathedral.

proven: not proven a verdict that the accused is probably
guilty but that evidence is insufficient; he or she is then
discharged unconditionally.

public room a room in a house which can be used for
entertaining guests, ie a sitting room, dining room.

puckle see **pickle**.

pudding a kind of sausage made with a mixture of animal entrails, blood, oatmeal etc.

puddock a frog; a toad.

puggie[1] a monkey. **fou as a puggie** very drunk

puggie[2] a hole into which marbles are rolled in a game; a fruit machine.

puir [payr, poe:r], (*North-East*) **peer** poor.

pun(d) a pound (in weight or money).

pursuer in Scots law, a person who brings an action in a civil case.

quaich a shallow two-handled drinking bowl, now usually of silver and used as a trophy etc.

quine, quinie (*mainly North-East*) a girl, lass, a young woman; a daughter.

radge violently excited, furious; sexually excited; silly, weak-minded.

ragnail a piece of loose skin at the base of a fingernail.

rammy a (loud) disturbance, a rumpus.

rasp a raspberry.

rax to stretch; to sprain.

rector the head teacher of some secondary schools; clergyman in charge of a Scottish Episcopal congregation. **the (Lord) Rector** a university official, now a public figure elected by the students.

redd to clear (out), tidy (up).

reek smoke. **Auld Reekie** nickname for Edinburgh.

reid red.

renaig to refuse to do something, shirk responsibility.

retiral retirement.

richt right.

Riding of the Marches or **Common Riding** an annual festival in certain towns, especially in the Borders, having its origin in the patrolling of the boundaries (**marches**) of the **burgh**.

rig the back or backbone; a ridge, long narrow hill; a raised strip of ploughed land.

rin run.

rone a roof gutter. **rone-pipe** the pipe which drains water from this.

roon round.

round steak a cut of beef from the hindquarter.

roup a sale or let by public auction.

rowie (*North-East*) a kind of rich flaky bread roll with a high fat content.

rump steak in Scotland, a cut of beef corresponding to English topside + silverside.

runkle wrinkle; crease, rumple.

sae so.

saft soft.

sair sore. **a sair fecht** a hard struggle.

sang a song.

sark a shirt.

Sassenach (an) English (person).

sax six.

scaffie a refuse-collector.

scheme or **housing scheme** a local-authority housing estate. **schemie** shabby, low-class.

Scots/Scotch/Scottish there is much confusion about the precise use of these words. Briefly, in general current usage in Scotland, **Scots** is usual, except when referring to national or official concepts, when **Scottish** is preferred: *Scottish politics, Scottish schools*, but *Scots law*; **Scotch** is used mainly to refer to items of food and drink. In addition to **Scotch** (**whisky**), examples include; **Scotch bun = black bun**; **Scotch broth** a thick vegetable soup made with mutton; **Scotch collops** thin slices of meat simmered in a sauce.

scrieve to write.

scunner *verb* to sicken; to disgust. *noun* a feeling of nausea or disgust; a thing which or person who causes this.

sea loch an arm of the sea.

seeven seven.

semmit a (man's) vest, undershirt.

session: Court of Session the highest civil court in Scotland. *See also* **kirk session.**

sgian dubh see **skean dhu.**

sharn dung.

shed *verb* to divide, separate. *noun* a parting in the hair.

sheltie a Shetland pony.

sheriff (1) (**sheriff principal**) the chief judge of an area. (2) a legal officer who can act as judge in most cases (both civil and criminal) in a **sheriff court. sheriff officer** an official who carries out the warrants of a **sheriff**, especially in regard to **poinding**, serves summonses etc.

sheuch [shooch] a ditch, drain, trench; a street gutter.

shieling a summer pasture; a rough hut on this.

shilpit thin, starved- or ill-looking.

shinty a hockey-like game, played by men, mainly in the Highlands.

shoogle to shake, rock, be or make unsteady. **shoogly** unsteady.

shot a brief use of something: *Have a shot of my bike.*

sic such.

siller money.

skail to disperse, scatter, separate.

skean dhu, *Gaelic* **sgian dubh** (meaning 'black knife') a knife or dagger worn in the stocking as part of Highland dress.

skelf a splinter, especially in the skin.

skellie(-eyed) squint-eyed.

skelp to slap, smack, spank.

skite to slide, slither; to (cause to) go off at an angle or
     in an odd direction; to strike, knock sharply.

skoosh *verb* to gush in spurts or splashes, squirt;
     to move about quickly. *noun* (1) a splash, spurt
     (of liquid). (2) a fizzy soft drink, (3) something
     very easy to do.

slaister *verb* to work or do something messily, especially
     in a liquid. *noun* a state of (wet) mess or muddle; a
     person in such a state.

slater a woodlouse.

sleekit smooth, sly, cunning, hypocritical.

slitter *verb* to do something messily and wetly. *noun*
     a wet mess; a messy person.

sma small. (**wee**) **sma hours** the very early morning
     hours.

smeddum energy, spirit, vigour.

smiddy a smithy.

smirr a light drizzle.

smit to infect, affect by contact. **get the smit** to be
     infected; to fall in love.

smolt, smowt a young salmon (before the **grilse** stage);
     (**smowt**) a small thing or person.

sneck a catch, latch of a door etc.

snell (*of wind etc*) cold and biting.

snib a catch or small bolt for a door etc.

sonsy healthily buxom, chubby, plumply attractive.

sort to mend, repair.

souch [sooch] a rushing or whizzing noise; a deep breath,
     a sigh. **keep a calm souch** to keep calm or quiet.

soutar [sootər] a cobbler, shoemaker.

spale-bone a shoulder cut of meat, blade-bone steak.

speir to ask (questions).

speug [spyug] a sparrow.

sporran a kind of purse or money-pouch worn in front
     of a kilt.

sprauchle, sprachle to move or climb clumsily and with
    effort.

spurtle a stick for stirring porridge etc.

stance a stopping place for vehicles, eg a taxi rank.

stane stone.

stank a street gutter; a grating over it.

stave to sprain (a joint).

stay to live, reside.

stishie see **stushie**.

stob a stake, (fence)post.

stook a small number of sheaves set up to dry in a field.

stookie plaster (of Paris); a plaster cast (for a broken
    limb); a plaster statue etc. *Don't just stand there like
    a stookie.*

stooshie see **stushie.**

stot[1] bounce. **stottin** drunk.

stot[2] a young ox, bullock.

stovies a dish of stewed potatoes, onions etc.

stour [stoor] dust, especially when flying in the air.

stramash a disturbance, uproar.

strath a broad valley.

stravaig to wander aimlessly; to go about a lot, enjoying
    oneself.

stushie, stooshie, stishie a fuss, commotion.

supper a meal of fish or meat with chips bought in a fish-
    and-chip shop: *fish supper, haggis supper, chicken
    supper.*

swallie *verb* to swallow. *noun* a swallow; an alcoholic
    drink

sweetie a sweet(meat). **sweetie-wife** a (gossipy)
    effeminate man.

sweir reluctant, unwilling, lazy.

swither to hesitate, dither, be uncertain what to do.

syboe, sybie a spring onion.

syne[1] then; since.

syne², **synd** to wash, rinse (perfunctorily).

synod a church court between the **presbytery** and the **General Assembly**.

syver a street-gutter; a grating over it.

tablet a kind of fudge, of a stiff, friable consistency.

tae¹ a toe.

tae² to; too.

tak to take. **tak tent** to pay head, take care.

tap top

tapsalteerie upside down, in a muddle, confusion.

tartan a kind of woollen cloth with a pattern of checks and stripes; such a pattern. Different patterns are regarded as belonging to particular families, but there is very little historical justification for this.

tattie a potato. **tattie-bogle** a scarecrow.

tawse a leather strap with thongs formerly much used for punishing schoolchildren.

tea, *also* **high tea** a main evening meal consisting of one cooked course, followed by bread, cakes, etc and tea. **teabread** semi-sweet buns etc. **tea jenny** a person (of either sex) who drinks a lot of tea.

tenement a block of flats, usually of three or four storeys.

teuch [tyooch] tough.

teuchter [**tyooch**tər] derogatory word for a Highlander or country person.

thae those.

that so. *I was that tired*.

thirled bound by some tie of duty, habit, affection etc.

thole to tolerate, endure, put up with.

thon see **yon**.

thrang busy.

thrapple the windpipe; the throat, gullet. **weet one's thrapple** to have a drink.

thraw to throw. **thrawn** stubborn, sullenly obstinate.

till to.

tint see **tyne.**

tolbooth a town hall; a town jail (now used only
   of certain buildings which formerly served these
   purposes).

town house a town hall.

trades (**holiday**) the annual industrial summer holiday in
   certain towns in the east of Scotland, eg in Edinburgh,
   the first two weeks of July. Compare **Fair.**

trauchled overburdened with work etc, harassed.

trews *originally* close-fitting, usually tartan trousers; *now*
   tartan trousers worn by some Scottish regiments; short
   tartan underpants worn under the kilt.

tryst *noun* an agreed meeting. *verb* to arrange a meeting.

tumshie a turnip; a fat vacant-looking person.

twa, twae two.

twal twelve.

tyne to lose. **tint** lost.

unco unusual, odd; extraordinary, great. **the unco guid**
   the self-righteously moral or pious.

Up-Helly-Aa a festival held in Lerwick, Shetland, at the end
   of January.

uplift to pick up, collect (passengers, parcels, money etc).

upset price eg at an auction sale, one which the seller
   would accept.

upstanding: be upstanding to get to one's feet, eg to
   drink a toast.

wabbit tired out, feeling feeble.

wae woe.

wallie ornamental, porcelain, china. **wallies** false teeth.
   wallie close a tiled entry (considered upmarket,
   especially in Glasgow). **wallie dug** one of a pair
   of ornamental china dogs.

wan see **ane.**

wan- un-.

warsle to wrestle, struggle.

wauk(en) to wak(en).

waulking song a Gaelic song formerly sung by Hebridean women while fulling cloth.

waur worse.

wean [wayn] (*mainly West*) a child.

wee small. **Wee Free** see **Free Church.**

weel well.

weet wet. **weet the bairn's head** to drink a toast to a newborn baby

wersh of food or drink, either tasteless, insipid or (*in some areas*) sour, harsh, bitter.

wha, whae, (*North-East*) **fa** who.

whan, (*North-East*) **fan** when.

whaup a curlew.

whaur, whar, (*North-East*) **far** where.

wheech [hweech] to move (through the air) with a whizzing sound, or very rapidly or suddenly.

wheen: a wheen a few.

wheesht stop your noise, be quiet. **haud yer wheesht** be quiet, don't say any more.

whigmaleerie a trifle, fanciful ornament.

whisky see p. 91.

whit, (*North East*) **fit** whit. **whit (or fit) like** what kind of. **fit like** (*used as greeting in the North-East*) how are you?

wi with.

wife, wifie a woman, now usually an older one.

windae a window.

wrang wrong.

yestreen yesterday (evening).

yett a gate.

yeukie itchy; eager; sexually aroused.

yin see **ane.**

yon, thon that (*indicating something at a distance*).

yowe a ewe.

GAELIC-ENGLISH

This brief list covers mainly Gaelic words and phrases in general use at the present time, and some words have been included because they occur frequently in place-names.

Gaelic grammar is a complicated subject and it is impossible to deal with it here in any depth at all. If you would like to know more about it, there are excellent course books and websites available; see list on pp. 93-4. The following brief notes may help a little in finding words in dictionaries and glossaries.

Gaelic words change in a number of ways to form the plural, feminine, genitive, dative and vocative case of nouns, past tense of verbs etc. Changes will be found at the beginning, at the end and also in the middle of a word. A common change at the beginning of a word is the insertion of *h* after a consonant and this alters the sound of the preceding letter (eg *bh* and *mh* and pronounced like English *v*, *ph* is pronounced *f*). Thus if you are looking for a word beginning with *bh, ch, dh, fh, gh, mh, ph, th,* look it up in the dictionary without the *h*.

Common plural forms include:

-an	as in	**eilean**,	plural	**eileanan**
-ichean	as in	**bàta**,	plural	**bàtaichean**
change of vowel	as in	**bòrd**,	plural	**bùird**

The definite article varies according to grammar and spelling, for example according to whether the word is masculine or feminine, singular or plural, and according to the first letter of the next word, eg:

masculine	**an cù**	the dog
	am balach	the boy
	a bhalaich	boy *(vocative case,* ie when talking to him)
	bàta a'bhalaich	the boy's boat
feminine	**a'chaileag**	the girl
	na caileig	of the girl
	na caileagan	the girls
	nan caileagan	of the girls

Gaelic spelling seems more complicated than it actually is, and it is in fact much more logical than English spelling. One reason for apparently unnecessary letters is the rule of 'broad to broad and narrow to narrow', ie a broad vowel (*a, o* or *u*) in one syllable must be balanced by a broad vowel in the syllable before or after it; likewise a narrow vowel (*e* or *i*) must be balanced by a narrow vowel. Thus in *uairean*, plural of *uair* (time, hour), the *e* is inserted to balance the *i* in the previous syllable.

a [ə] his, her, its.
abair [apər] to say.
abhainn [avinʸ] a river.
acair [achkər] an anchor.
ach [ach] but.
achadh [achəgh] a field.
acras [ahkras] hunger.
adhar [aoar] sky, air.
agus [agəs] and.
aig [ayk, ek] on.
aimsir [aməshir] weather; time.
ainm [anam] a name.
air [ayr] on. **air ais** [ayr ash] back(wards); ago. **air falbh** [ayr falav] away.

àird [a:rsht] height; promontory; direction.
airgead [arəkit] money; silver.
àirigh [a:ree] a **shieling**, summer pasture dwelling.
airson [ayrson] for.
aiseag [ashak] a ferry.
àite [a:tyə] a place.
Alba [alapə] Scotland.
Albannach [alapanoch] Scottish, Scots; a Scotsman.
allt [aoolt] a stream, small river.
àm [aoom] time.
a-mach [əmach] out, outwards.
am-maireach [əma:roch] tomorrow.
a-muigh [əmooee] out, outside.
an-dè [ən jay:] yesterday.
an-diugh [ən joo] today.
an-dràsda [ən dra:stə] now.
ann [aoon] in.
a nuas [ənooəs] down.
a-null [ənowl] over (to here).
aodann [oe:tan] a face.
aon [oen] one.
aonach [oe:nach] a hill; a ridge; a moor.
aosda [oe:stə] aged; ancient.
a-rithist [əree-isht^y] again.
a-staigh [əstY] in, inside; at home.
a-steach [əstyech] in, into.
aran [aran] bread.
arbhar [aravar] corn.
àrd [a:rt] high.
às [as] from, out of.
athair [ahər] a father.
bad [bat] a clump, tuft; a place, spot.
bàgh [ba:gh] a bay.
baile [balə] a town, village.
bainne [banyə] milk.

balach [**ba**loch] a boy.

ball [**ba**ool] a limb; a member: **Ball Pàrlamaid** [-**pa**:rlamat^y] Member of Parliament.

ball-coise [**ba**ool **ko**shə] football.

bàn [ba:n] white; fair.

ban(a)- [**ban**(a)] woman, female.

banacharaid [**ba**nacharaj] a (female) friend, relative.

banais [**ba**neesh] a wedding.

banaltram [**ba**naltrum] a nurse.

banrigh [**ba**ooree] a queen.

bàrd [ba:rt] a poet, bard.

bàrdachd [**ba**:rtochk] poetry.

bàrr [ba:r] the top of something; cream.

barrachd [**ba**rochk] more.

bàs [ba:s] death.

bata [**ba**tə] a stick.

bàta [**ba**:tə] a boat.

beag [bayk] small.

bealach [**bya**loch] a mountain pass.

bean [ben] a woman; a wife.

beannachd [**bya**nochk] a blessing.

beartach [**bya**rshtoch] rich.

beatha [**be**hə] life.

beinn [bYn] a mountain, hill.

beithe [**be**hə] a birch tree.

beò [byaw] alive.

beul [**bee**al] a mouth.

Beurla [**bayr**lə] English.

bha [va] was, were.

bho [vo] from.

biadh [**bee**əgh] food.

bidean [**bee**jən] a peak, summit.

binn [been^y] (*of sound*) sweet, melodious.

binnean [**bee**nyən] a high, pointed hill, a peak.

Biobull [**bee**:pul] the Bible.

birlinn [**bir**leen^y] a galley (ship.)

blàr [bla:r] a plain, a battlefield.

blas [blas] a taste, flavour.

blàth[1] [bla:] warm.

blàth[2] [bla:] blossom, bloom.

bliadhna [**blee**unə] a year. **Bliadhna Mhath Ùr** [- va **oo:r**] Happy New Year.

bò [boa:], *plural* **bà** [ba:] a cow.

bochd [bochk] poor.

bocsa [**bok**sə] a box; an accordeon.

bodach [**bo**toch] an old man.

bodhar [**boa**ər] deaf.

bog [boak] soft, limp. **bog fliuch** [- flyooch] soaking wet.

bòidheach [**bo:**yoch] beautiful.

boireannach [**bor**ənoch] a woman.

bonn [bown] base, bottom; sole (of foot); a coin; a medal.

bòrd [bawrsht] a table; a board.

bothan [**bo**han] a small (rough) hut; in the Island of Lewis, one for the illicit sale and consumption of liquor.

bracaist [**bra**kosht^y] breakfast.

bradan [**bra**tan] a salmon.

braigh [**bra**ee] the upper part; a brae.

bratach [**bra**toch] a flag, banner.

bràthair [**bra:**hir] a brother.

breac [brechk] *noun* a trout. *adjective* speckled, spotted.

breacan [**brech**kan] tartan.

breug [**bree**ak] lie.

briagha [**bree**a] beautiful.

brìgh [bree:] essence, substance; meaning; juice.

briogais [**bree**keesh] trousers.

briste [**breesh**tyə] broken.

brochan [**bro**chan] porridge, gruel.

bròg [brawk] a shoe.

brònach [**braw**noch] sad.

brosnaich [**bros**neech] to encourage.

bruach [**broo**uch] a bank (of a river etc); a slope; a border, edge.

bruadar [**broo**atər] dream.

bruidhinn [**bree**yeenʸ] speaking.

buachaille [**boo**uchəlyə] a shepherd, herdsman.

buain [**boo**anʸ] to reap, harvest.

buidhe [**boo**yə] yellow.

bun [**boon**] the bottom, base, foot; a rivermouth. **bun-sgoil** [**boon** skol] a primary school.

buntàta [boon**ta**:tə] potato.

bùrn [boo:rn] water.

bùth [boo:] a shop.

cabar [**ka**bar] a rafter; a caber; an antler.

cabhag [**ka**fak] hurry, haste.

cadal [**ka**tul] to sleep.

caileag [**ka**lak] a girl.

cailleach [**ka**lyoch] an old woman.

cainnt [**ka**eentʸ] speech.

cairteal [**kar**shtyal] a quarter.

càise [**ka**:shə] cheese.

Càisg: a' Chàisg [ə cha:**shk**] Easter.

caisteal [**kash**tyal] a castle.

càite [**ka**:tyə] where. **Càit'a bheil thu?** [**ka**:tyə **vayl** oo] Where are you?

caladh [**ka**la(gh)] harbour.

Callainn: a' Challain [ə cha**lin**ʸ], **oidhche Challainn** [**Y**chə -] traditionally the Old New Year (now 13 January), but now often Hogmanay, 31 December.

calltainn [**ka**ooltinʸ] a hazel tree.

calman [**ka**laman] a dove, pigeon.

cam [kowm] bent, crooked.

caman [**ka**man] a **shinty** stick.

camas [**ka**məs] a bay.

can [kan] to say, **can seo** [- **sho**] say this.

cànan [**ka**:nan] language.

caochail [**koe**chil^y] die.

caol [koe:l] narrow.

caora [**koe**:rə] a sheep.

caorann [**koe**:ran] a rowan tree.

caraid [**ka**rat^y] a friend.

càrn [ka:rn] a cairn, heap of stones; a rounded hill.

cas¹ [kas] a foot, leg. **cas-chrom** [kas **chrowm**] a foot-plough.

cas² [kas] steep.

cathair [**ka**hir] a chair; a city.

ceann [**kya**oon] a head. **ceann-suidhe** [- **soo**yə] a chairman, president.

cearc [kyerk] a hen.

ceàrr [kya:r] wrong; left-handed.

ceart [kyarsht] right.

ceartas [**kyarsh**təs] justice.

ceathrad [**kay**ret] forty (*in the new decimal counting system*).

cèilidh [**kay**lee] a social gathering; a concert.

ceist [kaysht] question

Cèitean: an Cèitean [ən **kay**:tyan] (the month of) May.

ceithir [**kay**hir] four. **ceithir fichead** [- **feech**ət] eighty (*in the traditional counting system by twenties*).
    ceithir fichead 's a deich [- sə **jay**ch] ninety (*in the traditional counting system by twenties*).

ceò [kyaw] mist.

ceòl [kyawl] music.

ceud [**kee**ət] a hundred.

ceum [kay:m] a step.

cha(n) [cha(n)] not.

chun [choon] to.

ciad [**kee**ət] first.

ciamar [**kyi**mər] how. **Ciamar a tha sibh?** [- ə **ha**: sheev] How are you?

cinnteach [**kyee**ntyoch] certain.

cìoch [**kee**och] a breast.

cìr [kee:r] a comb.

ciste [**kee**shtyə] a box, chest; a coffin.

clach [klach] a stone.

clachan [**kla**chan] a village round a church.

cladach [**kla**toch] a shore.

clann [**kla**oon] children.

clàr [kla:r] a record, disk.

clàrsach [**kla:r**soch] a harp.

clì [klee] left. **an làmh chlì** the left hand.

clò[1] [claw] print; a printing press.

clò[2] [claw] cloth, tweed.

cnoc [krochk] a hill.

cò [coa] who? **Cò tha sin?** who is that? **Cò as a tha sibh?** [coa as ə ha: sheev] Where are you from?

caogad [**koe**kət] fifty (in the new decimal counting system).

co-dhiù [co**yoo:**] however, nevertheless; anyway.

cogadh [**kok**əgh] war.

còig [**koa**ik] five.

coileach [**ku**loch] a cockerel.

coille [**ku**lyə] a wood.

còinneach [**koa:**nyoch] moss.

coinneamh [**ku**nyoo] a meeting.

coirce [**kork**ə] oats.

còisir [**kaw**shir] choir.

coire [**kor**ə] a cauldron; a kettle; a hollow in mountains, often near the top of a hill, a **corrie**.

colaiste [**ko**lashtyə] college.

coma [**koa**mə] indifferent. **coma co-dhiù** [- ko **yoo**:] couldn't care less.

comann, comunn [**koa**mən] an association, society, committee **An Comunn Gàidhealach** [ən - **gay**aloch] the Highland Association. **Comunn na Gàidhlig** [- nə **ga:**leek] Association for Gaelic.

comhairle [**kaw**ərlyə] advice, counsel; a council.
  Comhairle nan Eilean Siar [- nən yaylan **shee**ar]
  Western Isles Council. **Comhairle nan Sgoiltean**
  Àraich [- nən **skolt**yən **a**:reech] Association of Gaelic
  Nursery Schools and Playgroups.
còmhla [**kaw**lə] together. **còmhla ri** [- ree] with.
comunn see **comann.**
cothrom [**ko**rom] a chance, opportunity
còrr [kawr] more. **còrr is** [- is] more than.
crann [**kra**oon] a mast; a plough.
craobh [kroe:v] a tree.
craoladh [**kroe**:ləgh] broadcasting. **BBC Craoladh nan**
  Gàidheal [nan **gay**əl] the BBC Gaelic language service
creag [krayk] a rock.
cridhe [**kree**ə] the heart. **gràdh mo chridhe** [**gra:gh**
  mo **chree**ə] love of my heart.
crìoch [**kree**och] end, limit, boundary.
crodh [kroa] cattle.
croit [krot^y] a croft. **croitear** [**krot**yər] a crofter.
crom [krowm] bent, crooked.
cruach [**kroo**ach] a heap, stack.
cruinn [**kr**Yn^y] round.
cù [koo:] a dog.
cuan [**koo**an] an ocean.
cuid [koot^y] a portion, some.
cuideachd [**koot**yochk] also.
Cuimreach [**kim**əroch] Welsh; a Welsh person.
cuine [**koo**nyə] when?
cùl [koo:l] the back.
cùthag [**koo**ak] a cuckoo.
dà [da:] two. **dà-chànanach** [- **cha**:nanoch] bilingual.
dà fhichead [- **ee**chət] forty (*in the traditional counting*
  system by twenties). **dà-dheug** [- **ghee**uk] twelve.
dachaidh [**da**chee] home. **mo dhachaidh** [mo **gha**chee]
  my home.

dall [daool] blind.

damh [daf] a stag.

Dàmhair: an Dàmhair [ən da:vər] October.

dàn [da:n] a poem, song.

dàna [da:nə] bold, cheeky.

danns [daoons] dance.

darach [daroch] an oak tree.

dath [da] colour.

de[1] [je] of.

dè[2] [jay:] what. **Dè tha sin?** [- ha shin] What is that?

deagh [jay] good. (see **dùrachd**).

dealain [jalanʸ] electricity.

dealbh [jalav] a picture. **dealbh-chluich** [- chlooeech]
    a play.

dèan [jceən] to do, make.

dearbh: gu dearbh [goo jerav] indeed.

dearg [jerak] red.

deas [jes] south; right(-hand).

deich [jaych] ten. **deich air fhichead** [- ər eechət]
    thirty (in the traditional counting system by twenties).

dèidh: an dèidh [ən jay:] after.

deireadh [jayrəgh] end. **deireadh an là** [- an la:] end
    of the day.

deoch [joch] (a) drink.

dha [gha] to him.

dhi [ghee] to her.

dhomh [gho] to me.

dia [jeeə] god.

diabhal [jeeə-al] devil.

Diardaoin [jərdoe:nʸ] Thursday.

Diciadaoin [jəkeeatinʸ] Wednesday.

Didòmhnaich [jədawneech] Sunday.

Dihaoine [jəhoe:nyə] Friday.

dìleas [jee:ləs] faithful, loyal.

Diluain [jəlooanʸ] Monday.

Dimairt [jəma:rsht^y] Tuesday.

dìollaid [jee:əlat^y] a saddle.

dìreach [jee:roch] straight; exactly.

dìreadh [jee:rəgh] a climb, ascent.

Disathurna [jəsahurnə] Saturday.

do¹ [do] your *(singular)*, 'thy' (see **thu**).

do² [do] to.

dòbhran [doa:ran] an otter.

dòchas [dawchas] hope.

doire [dirə] a thicket, clump of trees.

dona [donə] bad, evil.

donn [down] brown.

doras [dorəs] a door.

dorch [doroch] dark.

dragh [droegh] trouble.

droch [droch] bad.

drochaid [drochat^y] a bridge.

druim [droeeem, drim] the back; a ridge.

dualchas [doouləchəs] heritage, tradition.

dubh [doo] black.

Dùbhlachd: an Dùbhlachd [ən doo:lochk]
    December.

dùil [doo:l] expectation.

duilich [dooleech] sorry.

dùin [doo:n^y] shut. **Dùin an doras** [- ən dorəs] Shut the
    door.

duine [dinyə] a man.

dùn [doo:n] a fort.

dùrachd: leis gach deagh dhùrachd [laysh gach jay
    ghoo:rochk] with every good wish.

dùsgadh [doo:skəgh] waking.

dùthaich [doo:eech] a country.

e [e] he; him; it.

each [ech] a horse.

eachdraidh [yechktree] history.

eadar [**ay**tar] between. **an t-eadar-lìon** [ən **tayt**ar-lyeeən] the internet. **eadar-nàiseanta** [aytar-**na:**shantə] international.

eag [ayk] a nick, notch. **eagach** [**ayk**och] notched, jagged.

eagal [**ayk**əl] fear.

eaglais [**ayk**lish] a church.

eala [**yal**ə] a swan.

ealain [**yal**an^y] art.

ear [er] east.

earb [**er**əp] a roe deer.

earrach [**yar**och] spring, the season.

eas [es] a waterfall.

easbuig [**es**pik] a bishop.

eile [**ayl**ə] other.

eilean [**ayl**an] an island.

eilid [**ayl**it^y] a hind.

Èireannach [**ay:**ranoch] Irish; an Irish person.

èirich [**ay:**reech] to rise.

èisd [ay:sht^y] to listen.

eòlas [**yawl**əs] knowledge.

eòrna [**yawr**nə] barley.

Eòrpa [**yawr**pə] Europe.

eudail: m'eudail [**may:**tal^y] my darling (*often to a child*).

eug [ay:k] death.

eun [ay:n], *plural* **eòin** [yawn^y] a bird.

facal [**fach**kal] a word.

faclair [**fach**klar] a dictionary.

fada [**fat**ə] long.

fàg [fa:k] to leave. **fàgail** [**fa:**kal^y] leaving.

fàilte [**fa:l**tyə] welcome.

faing [fYnk^y] a fank, sheep-pen.

fàinne [**fa:**nyə] a ring.

faisg air [**fashk** ayr] near.

falbh [**fal**av] to leave.

falt [falt] hair.

fann [**fa**oon] weak.

faochag [**foe**chak] a whelk.

faoileag [**foe**:lak] a seagull.

Faoilteach: am Faoilteach [əm **foe**:ltyoch]: January.

far [far] where.

farpais [**far**pish] a competition.

fàs[1] [fa:s] to grow.

fàs[2] [fa:s] empty, unoccupied, deserted.

fàsach [**fa**:soch] a deserted place, wilderness.

fasgach [**fas**koch] sheltered, protected.

feadag [**fe**tak] a whistle (the instrument); a plover.

feadan [**fe**tan] a (bagpipe) chanter.

feumainn [**fe**min[y]] seaweed.

fear [fer] a man; (*when referring to a masculine person or thing*) one. **fear an taigh** [- ən tehə] the chairman of a social gathering such as a **ceilidh**.

feasgar [**fays**kər] evening. **feasgar math** [- ma] good evening.

fèill [fay:l[y]] a festival, fair, market, sale.

fèis [fay:sh] a festival.

feòil [fyaw:l[y]] meat.

feòrag [**fya**wrak] a squirrel.

feum [faym] need.

feur [**fee**ar] grass.

fiacail [**fee**uchkil[y]] a tooth.

fiadh [**fee**ugh] a deer.

fichead [**fee**chət] twenty.

fidheall [**fee**yəl] a fiddle, violin.

fileanta [**fee**ləntə] fluent.

fiodh [fyigh] wood.

fion [**fee**un] wine.

fionn [fyown] white, pale-coloured.

fior [fee:r] true.

fios [fees] knowledge, information.
Fir Chlis [feer chleesh]: **na Fir Chlis** the Aurora
  Borealis, the Northern Lights.
fitheach [feeoch] a raven.
fliuch [flyooch] wet.
fo [fo] under.
foghar [foaur] autumn.
foghlam [foelum] learning, education.
foillsich [fŶlsheech] to show; to make public; to publish.
fonn [fown] a tune.
fosgail [foaskil^y] to open.
Frangach [fraoonkoch] French; a French person.
fraoch [froe:ch] heather.
fras [fras] a shower.
frìth [free:] a deer forest (*now usually a treeless area*).
fuaim [fooaeem] sound, noise.
fuar [foour] cold.
fuaran [foouran] a well, spring; a fountain.
fuil [fool^y] blood.
furasda [foorəstə] easy.
gach [gach] each.
Gàidheal [gayal] a Highlander, Gael.
Gàidhealach [gayəlach] Highland.
Gàidhealteachd [gayəltochk] Highlands.
Gàidhlig [ga:leek] Gaelic
gainmheach [ganavoch] sand.
gàire [ga:rə] a laugh.
gairm [girim] a call; a cockcrow.
gaisgeach [gashkoch] a hero.
Gall [gaool] a Lowlander.
gallda [gaooltə] foreign; **Gallda** Lowland.
Galltachd [gaooltochk] the Lowlands.
gaol [goe:l] love.
gaoth [goe:] a wind.
garbh [garav] rough.

gàrradh [**ga:**rəgh] a garden; a (stone) wall, dyke.

gath [ga] a beam, ray (of light); a dart, barb, sting.

geal [gyal] white.

gealach [**gya**loch] the moon.

geamhradh [**gya**oorəgh] winter.

Gearmailteach [**gya**raməltyoch] German; a German (person).

Gearran: an Gearran [ən **gya**ran] February.

geàrr [gya:r] *adjective* short. *verb* to cut.

geug [gayk] a branch.

geur [**gee**ar] sharp.

Giblean: an Giblean [ən **gee**plən] April.

gille [**gee**lyə] a boy, young man. **gille-Caluim** [- **cha**lim] sword dance.

giomach [**gee**moch] a lobster.

giuthas [**gyoo**əs] fir, pine.

glac [glachk] a hollow, narrow valley.

glan [glan] clean.

glas [glas] grey, greenish-grey, green.

glè [glay] very. **glè mhath** [- **va**] very good.

gleann [**gla**oon] a (narrow) valley, **glen**.

glic [gleechk] wise, sensible.

gob [goap] a beak; (*informal*) the mouth.

gobha [**goa**ə] a blacksmith.

gobhar [**goa**ər] a goat.

goirid [**gir**it^y] short.

gòrach [**gaw:**roch] stupid, foolish.

gorm [**gor**om] blue; (of grass, leaves etc) green.

gràdh [gra:] love.

grian [**gree**an] the sun.

gruamach [**groo**amoch] gloomy.

gu [goo] to; until. **gu bràth** [- **bra:**] for ever. **gu dearbh** [- **dye**rav] indeed. **gu leòir** [- **lyawr**] plenty. **gu math** [- **ma**] well.

gun [goon] without.

guth [goo] a voice.

hòro-geallaidh [hoaroa **ya**lee] a (wild) party,
    celebration.

i [ee] she, her.

iad [eeət] they.

iar [eeər] west.

iarann [eeərən] iron.

iasg [eeəsk] a fish.

iasgair [eeəskir] a fisherman.

ifrinn [eefrinʸ] hell.

ìm [ee:m] butter.

inbhir [inəvər] a river-mouth.

inneal [eenyal] a machine, engine, instrument.

innis[1] [eeneesh] *verb* to tell.

innis[2] [ceneesh] *noun* a meadow; an island.

iolair [**yoo**lar] an eagle.

iomadh [iməgh] many (a).

ionad [inat] a place; a centre: **ionad slàinte** [- **sla:**ntyə]
    health centre.

ionnsaich [**yown**seech] to learn.

ìre [ee:rə] level, grade, stage; maturity.

iris [eerish] a magazine

is[1] [is] is, are.

is[2] [is] and (*short for* **agus**).

isean [eeshan] a chicken.

iubhar [**yoo**ər] a yew tree.

Iuchar: an t-Iuchar [ən **tyoo**chər] July.

lach [lach] a wild duck.

lag[1] [lak] *adjective* weak.

lag[2] [lak] *noun* a hollow.

làidir [**la:**tyir] strong.

laigh [lY] to lie (down).

làirig [**la:**rik] a mountain pass.

làmh [la:v] a hand.

làn [la:n] full.

laoch [loe:ch] hero.

laogh [loegh] a calf.

làr [la:r] a floor.

làrach [**la:**roch] a site; a ruin.

latha [**la:**] a day. **laithean-saora** [**l**Yən-**soe:**rə] holidays.

le [le] with, belonging to; by.

leabaidh [**lye**pee] a bed.

leabhar [**lyo**ər] a book.

leabharlann [**lyo**ərlown] a library.

leac [lyechk] a flat stone, slab.

leanabh [**lye**nəv] a (small) child, a baby.

leann [lyown] beer, ale.

leannan [**lye**nan] a lover, sweetheart.

leathann [**lye**hən] broad.

leig [lyik] to let, allow.

lèine [**lay**nyə] a shirt.

lèirsinn [**lyayr**sheen^y] sight, vision.

leis [laysh] with (the), with him, with it.

leisgeul [**lyaysh**kal] an excuse, apology. **gabh mo leisgeul!** [gav moa -] excuse me!

leth [lye] half. **leth-cheud** [- chit] fifty. **leth-uair** [- ər] half an hour.

leum [laym] (a) leap.

liath [**lyee**ə] grey, bluish-grey.

lighiche [**lyee**eechə] doctor, physician.

linn [leen^y] a century.

linne [**lyee**nyə] a pool; a waterfall.

lìon [**lyee**ən] a net.

litir [**lyee**tyir] a letter.

loch [loch] a loch, lake. **lochan** [**lo**chan] a little loch.

Lochlannach [**loch**lanoch] a Scandinavian, now a Norwegian.

lom [lowm] bare.

lòn[1] [lawn] food.

lòn[2] [lawn] a meadow, a marsh.

lon-dubh [lon **doo**] a blackbird.

long [lowng] a ship.

lorg [**lor**ak] a track, trace.

luaidh: a luaidh [ə loo**Y**] (my) darling.

luath [looə] fast, quick, swift.

lùb [loo:p] a bend.

luch [looch] a mouse.

luchd [loochk] people. **luchd-turuis** [- **too**reesh] tourists.

Lùnastal: an Lùnastal [ən **loo**:nəstal] August.

lus [loos] a plant.

mac [machk] a son.

machair [**ma**chir] a low-lying fertile plain; a sandy field behind a beach.

madadh [**ma**təgh] a dog; an animal of the dog family: **madadh-allaidh** [- **a**lee] a wolf; **madadh-ruadh** [- **roo**əgh] a fox.

madainn [**ma**tin^y] morning.

Màigh: a' Mhàigh [ə v**Y**:] May (the month).

maighdean [m**Y**tyin] a maiden.

maighstir [m**Y**shtyər] master; Mr.

màm [ma:m] a large rounded hill.

maol [moe:l] *adjective* bald, bare. *noun* a (rounded) headland, promontory.

mar [mar, mər] as, like. **mar sin** [- **shin**] like that.

marag [**ma**rak]: **marag dhubh** [- **ghoo**] black pudding. **marag gheal** [- **ghyal**] white pudding.

marbh [**ma**rav] dead.

Màrt: am Màrt [ə ma:rsht] March.

math [ma] good. **'s math sin** [sma **shin**] that's good.

màthair [**ma**:hir] a mother.

meadhan [**mee**an] middle.

meal do naidheachd! [myal tə **na**yochk] congratulations!

meall [**mya**ool] a lump, heap; a rounded hill.

meanbhchuileag [menə **chool**ak] midge.

measg: am measg [ə **maysk**] among.

meur [**mee**ər] a finger; a branch.

mi [mee] I, me.

mi- [mee] not, un-.

mil [meel] honey.

mìle [**mee**:lə] a thousand; a mile.

milis [**mee**leesh] sweet

ministear [**mee**neeshtyar] a minister.

mìos [**mee**:əs] a month.

mise [**mee**shə] I, me (*emphatic*).

mo [moa] my.

moch [moch] early.

mòd [mawt] a festival of Gaelic song, music and poetry.

mòine [**mawn**yə] peat.

moladh [**mol**əgh] praise.

monadh [**mon**əgh] a hill, mountain; a range; a moor.

mòr [moa:r] big.

mòran [**moa**:ran] much, a lot, many.

mu [moo] about, around.

muc [moochk] a pig.

muileann [**moo**lan] a mill.

muir [moor] the sea.

mullach [**moo**loch] a summit, hilltop.

na [na, nə] the (*plural*); of the (*feminine*).

nach [nach] that … not; which … not; who … not.

naidheachd [**na**yochk] news.

nàiseanta [**na**:shəntə] national

nan [nən] of the (*plural*).

naochad [**noe**chət] ninety (*in the new decimal counting system*).

naoi [noey] nine.

naomh [noe:v] *adjective* holy, sacred. *noun* a saint.

neach [nyech] a person. **neach-obrach** [-**oap**roch] a worker.

nead [nyet] a nest.

neo- [nyo] un-, not.

neo see **no**.

neònach [**nyaw**noch] strange.

neoni [**nyo**nee] nothing, zero.

neul [nyeeəl] a cloud.

nighean [**nyee**ən], (*as part of name*) **nic** [nyeechk] a daughter.

nis: a nis [əneesh] now.

no, neo [no, nyo] or.

nochd[1] [nochk] a night.

nochd[2] [nochk] to show.

Nollaig [**no**lek^y] Christmas. **Nollaig Chridheil** [- **chree**əl] Merry Christmas.

nòta [**no**:tə] a pound (note).

nuadh [**noo**əgh] new.

nuair [**noo**ar] when.

o [o] from.

òb [awp] a bay

obair [**oa**pər] work.

ochd [oachk] eight. **ochdad** [**oachk**ət] eighty (*in the new decimal counting system*).

odhar [**oa**ər] dun-coloured, fawnish brown.

òg [awk] young. **an t-Òg-mhios** [ən **tawk**veeəs] June.

ogha [**oa**ə] a grandchild.

oidhche [Ychə] a night.

oifis [**o**feesh] an office. **oifis a' phuist** [ofeesh ə **foosht**^{y}] post office.

oilthigh [**ol**hY] a university.

oir[1] [or] for, because.

oir[2] [or] an edge.

òl [awl] to drink.

ola [**ol**ə] oil.

olc [olk] evil.

ollamh [oləv] (*mainly in titles*) professor, (non-medical) doctor. **An t-Ollamh MacIain** Gaelic name for Dr Johnson.

òr [awr] gold.

òraid [awratʸ] a speech.

òran [awran] a song.

òrd [awrt] a hammer.

os cionn [os kyoo:n] above.

ospadal [ospətal] a hospital.

pàigh [pY:] to pay.

pàipear [pe:pir] paper. **paipear naidheachd** [- nayochk] a newspaper.

pàrlamaid [pa:rlamatʸ] parliament.

partan [parshtan] a crab.

pathadh [pahəgh] thirst.

peann [pyaoon] a pen.

pìob [pee:p] a pipe; bagpipe. **pìob-mhòr** [-peep voa:r] the bagpipe.

pìobaire [pee:pərə] a piper.

pìobaireachd [pee:pərochk] pipe music; **pibroch** (*see Scots section*).

piuthar [pyooər] a sister.

pòg [pawk] kiss.

poileas [polis] police.

poll [powl] a pool; a hole; mud.

port[1] [porsht] a port; a landing place on the shore for small boats. **port-adhair** [- aoər] an airport.

port[2] [porsht] a tune. **port-a-beul** [- ə beeal] mouth-music.

pòs [paws] to marry. **pòsta** [pawstə] married.

prìomh [preeəv] prime. **prìomh mhinistear** [- veeneeshtyar] prime minister.

prìs [pree:sh] a price.

pùnnd [pownt] a pound (in weight or money).

raineach [ranyoch] fern; bracken.

rann [**ra**oon] a verse.

raoir: an raoir (ən **roeyr**) last night.

raon [roe:n] a field, plain, area. **raon-ola** [- olə] an oilfield

rathad [**ra**ət] a road. **rathad-iarainn** [- **ee**ərin^y] a railway.

reamhar [**ra**wir] fat.

reic [raychk] to sell.

rèidio [**ray:**dyoa] radio.

reul [ray:l] a star.

ri [ree] to.

riabhach [**ree**əvoch] brindled, striped or spotted.

riaghaltas [**ree**əltəs] government. **Riaghaltas na h-Alba** [- nə **ha**lapə] the Scottish Executive.

riamh [**ree**əv] ever.

rìbhinn [**ree**:veen^y] a maiden.

rìgh [ree:] a king.

rìoghachd [**ree**:ochk] a country, kingdom.

rionnag [**roo**nak] star.

ris [reesh] to (the), to him, to it.

ro [ro] too; very.

roimh, ro [roy, ro] before.

roinn [rYn^y] a share, section; a divison, department, region. **an Roinn Eòrpa** [ə rin-**yawr**pə] Europe.

ròn [rawn] a seal.

ros[1] [ros] a promontory.

ròs[2] [raws] a rose.

ruadh [**roo**əgh] red, brownish red, red-brown.

rubha [**roo**ə] a headland, promontory.

rud [root] a thing.

rugadh [**roo**kəgh] was born.

rùnaire [**roo:**narə] a secretary.

sabaid [**sa**pat^y] to fight, struggle.

Sàbaid [**sa:**pat^y] Sabbath. **latha na Sàbaid** [la nə -] Sunday.

sabhal [**soa**əl] a barn
sagart [**sa**kart] a priest.
saighdear [**sY**tyər] a soldier.
sàil [sa:l] a heel; a rounded hill.
salach [**sa**loch] dirty.
salann [**sa**lan] salt.
salm [**sa**lam] a psalm.
sàmhach [**sa**:voch] quiet.
samhradh [**sa**oorəgh] summer.
Samhain: an t-Samhain [ən ta**vin**ʸ] November. **Oidhche
    Shamhna** [Ychə **how**nə] Halloween.
sanas [**sa**nas] an advertisement; a hint; a whisper.
saoghal [**soe**hal] world.
saor[1] [soe:r] a joiner, carpenter.
saor[2] [soe:r] free.
Sasannach [**sa**sənoch] English; an English person.
seachd [**shechk**] seven. **seachdad** [**shech**kət] seventy (*in
    the new decimal counting system*)
seachdainn [**shech**kinʸ] a week.
seadh [**shoegh**] yes, indeed.
seall [**sha**ool] to look (at). **seall seo** [- **sho**] look at this.
sean [shen] old.
seanair [**she**nar] a grandfather.
seanchaidh [**she**nachee] a teller of traditional Gaelic
    stories.
seanmhair [**she**nevər] a grandmother.
seasgad [**shes**kət] sixty (*in the new decimal counting
    system*).
seileach [**shay**loch] willow.
seinn [shYn] to sing.
seirbhis [**she**rəvish] service.
seo [sho] this. **an seo** [ən **sho**] here.
seòl [shawl] sail.
seòladair [**shawl**ədayr] sailor.
seòrsa [**shawr**sə] a kind, sort.

sgadan [**ska**tan] a herring.

sgarbh [**ska**rav] cormorant.

sgeilp [**ska**ylp] a shelf.

sgeul [**skee**əl] a story.

sgian [**skee**ən] a knife.

sgiath [**skee**ə] a wing.

sgillinn [**skee**leen^y] a penny.

sgìre [**skee**:rə] a district; a parish.

sgìth [skee:] tired.

sgoil [skol] a school.

sgòr(r) [skawr] a sharp, steep rock or hill.

sgrìobh [skree:v] to write.

sguab [**skoo**ap] *noun* a sheaf; a brush, broom. *verb* to sweep.

sguir [skoor] to stop.

sgùrr [skoo:r] a sharp, steep rock or hill.

sia [**shee**ə] six.

sian [**shee**ən] a storm.

siar [**shee**ər] west(ern).

sibh [sheev] you (*plural and polite form – compare* vous *in French*).

sìde [**shee**:tyə] weather.

sin [shin] that. **an sin** [ən -] there.

sìn [shee:n] to stretch (out).

sinn [sheen^y] we. us.

sinnsear [**seen**shər] an ancestor.

sionnach [**shi**noch] a fox.

siorrachd [**shi**rochk] a county, shire.

sìth [shee:] peace.

sìthean [**shee**:hən] a hillock, fairy hill.

sìthiche [**shee**:eechə] a fairy.

siubhail [**shoo**əl^y] to travel.

siucar [**shooch**kar] sugar.

siud [shoot] that (*indicating something at a distance*).

slàinte [**sla:**ntyə] health. **slàinte mhath!** [- **va**] good health!, cheers!

slàn [sla:n] healthy; whole, complete.

slaodach [**sloe:**toch] slow.

slat [slaht] a rod.

sliabh [**shlee**əv] a hill(side), slope, moor.

slighe [**shlee**yə] a path, way.

sliochd [shlichk] descendants.

sloc(hd) [slochk] a pit, hollow.

sloinneadh [**slu**nyəgh] genealogy; surname.

smeòrach [**smyaw**roch] a thrush.

snàmh [sna:v] to swim.

sneachd(a) [**shnechk**(ə)] snow.

snog [snok] nice, pretty.

soilleir [**soel**yar] clear, bright.

soisgeul [**sosh**gal] gospel.

solas [**sol**əs] light.

sòlas [**saw**las] happiness, joy.

sonas [**son**əs] happiness.

sònraichte [**so:**reechtyə] particular, special.

soraidh [**sor**ee] farewell.

spàin [spa:nʸ] a spoon.

spèis [spay:sh] affection, regard.

speur [spayr] sky, space.

spiorad [**spir**at] spirit.

spòg [spawk] a paw, claw.

sporan [**spor**an] a purse, **sporran** (*see Scots section*).

sprèidh [spray:] cattle.

sràid [stra:tʸ] a street.

srath [stra] a broad river valley, strath.

sròn [strawn] a nose; a promontory, point of land.

srùpag [**stroo:**pak] a cup (of tea etc); literally 'slurp'.

sruth [stroo] a steam.

stad [stat] stop.

steall [**stya**ool] a gush, spout.

stiùiriche [**styoo:**reechə] a director.

stob [stop] a stake, pointed stick; a stump; a pointed hill.

stòr [stawr] a store. **stòr-dàta** [- **da:**tə] a database.

stùc(hd) [stoo:chk] a steep conical hill or peak.

suas [**soo**əs] up.

sùgh [soo:] juice.

suidh [sooy] to sit.

sùil [soo:l] an eye.

Sultain(n): **an t-Sultain(n)** [ən **tool**tin[y]] September.

taigh [tY] a house. **taigh-bidh** [- **bee:**] a restaurant.
    taigh-òsta [- **aws**tə] a hotel. **taigh-seinnse**
    [- **shYn**shə] a bar, pub, inn. **taigh-tasgaidh**
    [- **tas**kee] a museum.

talamh [**tal**av] earth, land, soil.

tana [**tan**ə] thin.

taobh [toc:v] side. **ri taobh** [ree **toev**] beside.

tapadh leat [**tap**ə leht], (*plural and polite form –*
    see **sibh**) **tapadh leibh** [**tap**ə **lYv**] thank you.

tarbh [**tar**av] a bull.

tàrmachan [**ta:r**mochan] a ptarmigan.

tarsainn [**tar**shin[y]] across.

tè [tyay] a woman, (*when referring to a feminine person
    or thing*) one.

teagaisg [**tyu**kisk] to teach.

teagamh [**tyu**kəv] doubt.

teaghlach [**tyao**loch] a family.

teanga [**tyoe**ghə] tongue.

teas [tyes] heat.

teine [**tyay**nyə] fire.

telebhisean [tele**vee**shan] television.

teth [tye] hot.

tha [ha] is, are, am.

thairis [**ha**reesh] over, across.

thall [howl] (over) there. **thall's a bhos** [- sə **vos**] here
    and there. **thall thairis** [-**ha**reesh] abroad.

thar [har] over.

thu, tu [oo:, too] you (*familiar form – compare tu in French*).

tì [tee] tea.

tìde [**tyee:**tyə] time.

tighearna [**tyee**ərnə] lord.

till [tyee:lʸ] to come back, return.

tioram [**tyi**rəm] dry.

timcheall [**tyi**meechal] about.

tìr [tyee:r] land. **tìr-mòr** [- **moa:r**] mainland.

tiugainn [**tyoo**kinʸ] come on.

tobar [**toa**par] a well.

tog [toak] to lift; to build.

toilichte [**to**leechtyə] pleased, happy.

toiseach [**to**shoch] beginning.

toll [towl] a hole, cavity.

tom [towm] a hillock.

tonn [town] a wave.

tòrr [tawr] a steep conical hill or rock.

tràigh [**tra:**ee] a shore.

trang [trang] busy.

tràth [tra:] early.

trì [tree:] three. **trì fichead** [- **fee**chət] sixty (*in the traditional counting system by twenties*). **trì fichead 's a deich** [- sə **dyaych**] seventy (*in the traditional counting system by twenties*).

trithead [**tree**hət] thirty (*in the new decimal counting system*).

tric [treechk] often.

triubhas [**troo**əs] trousers, trews.

tro, troimh [tro, troy] through.

trom [trowm] heavy.

trosg [trosk] cod.

truagh [**troo**əgh] poor, in a bad condition.

tu see **thu**.

tuath [tooə] north.

tuathanach [tooəhanoch] a farmer.

tubaist [toopasht] accident.

tulach [toolach] a (smallish) hill.

tunnag [toonak] a domestic duck.

turas [toorəs] a journey.

uachdar [ooəchkar] the top, upper part; cream.

uaine [ooanyə] green.

uair [ooər] an hour; time. **an uair** [ən ooər] when. **Dé an uair a tha e?** [dyay ən - ə ha e] What time is it?

uamh [ooav] a cave.

uamhasach [oo:avəsoch] awful(ly).

uan [ooan] a lamb.

uasal [ooəsal] noble.

ubhal [ooul] an apple.

ud [oot] that (*indicating something at a distance*).

ugh [oo] an egg.

ùghdaras [oo:tərəs] authority.

uile [oolə] every, all.

ùine [oo:nyə] time.

uinneag [oonyak] a window.

uirsgeul [oorshkyal] fable, novel.

uiseag [ooshak] a lark.

uisge [ooshkə] water; rain. **uisge-beatha** [- bchə] whisky.

ullamh [oolav] ready.

ùr [oo:r] new.

ùrlar [oo:rlar] a floor; (*in bagpipe music*) the (main) theme of a **pibroch**.

ùrnuigh [oo:rnee] a prayer.

urramach [oorəmoch] honourable. **an t-Urramach** [ən toorəmoch] the Reverend.

67

SCOTTISH PLACE-NAMES

Scottish place-names come from many different sources. Some, especially river names, come from sources of which there is now no provable explanation, some possibly from languages which have left no other trace. But the most striking aspect of Scottish names is the large number which are of Gaelic origin; some are even found in the south-eastern part of the country, which may never have been entirely Gaelic-speaking. Many of these names are obscured by strange spellings, owing to the fact that the majority of early mapmakers and other recorders were not familiar with Gaelic. They wrote the names down as they heard them, resulting in anglicized forms such as Balmore for *Bail(e) mòr* (the big village). Alternatively, they read them in a genuine Gaelic source, pronounced these names according to English pronunciation and wrote down the result of that.

Another rich source of place-names is Old Norse, especially names from the time of the Norse invasions from the 9th to the 13th century of the Northern and Western Isles and the adjoining seaboard. In the Western Isles and West Coast they are often in a strongly Gaelicized form. In Shetland and Orkney, where Norse domination lasted longer, names are predominantly from this source, and fair numbers of Scandinavian names are found in other areas, especially in the south-west.

Older strata of names include the Celtic language of the pre-Roman inhabitants (related to modern Welsh and Breton), variously called British, Brittonic, Brythonic and now often known as Cumbric. From the 7th century on Old English names were brought north with the Angles. The Picts, the mysterious people who ruled eastern Scotland north of the Forth from about the 3rd to the 9th century, have also left their mark on place-names; their language is believed to have been Celtic and the most prominent place-name element from it is *pit-*. Many names from more recent centuries are of course from Scots or English words and are thus more easily recognizable.

Very frequent mispronunciations of Scottish place-names arise from the different structures of these languages: in the Celtic languages (which include Gaelic, Cumbric and Pictish), the naming element comes first, the describing element second, whereas in the Germanic languages (which include Scots, English and Old Norse), the other way round. Place-names naturally put the stress on the describing element, thus Gaelic Beinn an **Eòin** (literally mountain of the bird) would become in English **Bird** Mountain. Frequently Celtic(-origin) names are thus pronounced with the wrong stress, for example **Cairn**gorms, instead of Cairn**gorms**, **Ab**erdeen, instead of Aber**deen**, **Avie**more, instead of Avie**more**.

Two notes on Older Scots spelling may be helpful:

> *z* sometimes represents Older Scots letter ȝ (yogh), which was pronounced roughly like the *y* sound in English 'million'. In some names, e.g. *Lenzie*, the *z* is now pronounced as in English, but in others, e.g. *Dalrulzion* [dal**ril**yən], the old pronunciation is retained;
>
> *quh-* is an Older Scots form of *wh-*, as in *Balquhidder* [bal**whi**dər].

The following is a very brief list of common place-name elements, where necessary referring back to the Scots-English or Gaelic-English sections. Some other place-names elements will be found in the Scots and Gaelic sections.

For further information see list of books and websites on p. 95.

a from *Old Norse* **á** a river.

-a see **-ey**.

aber *Pictish* or *Cumbric* a rivermouth.

ach, auch [ach, och] from *Gaelic* **achadh** a field.

-aig often represents *Old Norse* **vík** a bay, as in *Arisaig* Ari's bay.

a(i)rd *Gaelic* = a height.

alt see **ault**.

annat, annet from *Old Gaelic* **annaid** a church, mother church.

ardan, arden from *Gaelic* **àird** a height; a point of land; the ending is from *Gaelic* **an** meaning 'of the'.

auch see **ach**.

auchan, auchen [ochən] from *Gaelic* **achadh** a field; the ending is from *Gaelic* **an** meaning 'of the'.

auchter, ochter from *Gaelic* **uachdar** the surface, top; upper part.

a(u)lt [olt] from *Gaelic* **allt** a stream.

-ay see **-ey**.

bal, bally from *Gaelic* **baile** a town, village.

balloch, belloch from *Gaelic* **bealach** a mountain pass; but **Balloch** [baloch] near Inverness is **Bail' an Loch** the village on the loch.

ban(e) from *Gaelic* **bàn** white, light-coloured, fair.

bar(r) from *Gaelic* **bàrr** the top.

beg from *Gaelic* **beag** small.

belloch see **balloch**.

ben from *Gaelic* **beinn** a mountain, hill.

-bie, -by from *Old Norse* **býr** a farm, village.

blair from *Gaelic* **blàr** a field, a battlefield.

-bost, -bister, -bster, -boll, -poll, -pool are all reduced forms of *Old Norse* **bólstaðr** a farm, farmstead, homestead, dwelling place.

breck from *Gaelic* **breac** speckled, spotted; a trout.

bun *Gaelic* = the foot; a rivermouth.

-by see **-bie.**

caer *Cumbric* a fort.

cairn from *Gaelic* **càrn** a heap of stones.

calder a stream name from ancient Celtic meaning 'hard
water'.

cambus from *Gaelic* **camas** a bay.

car there are several possible sources, including *Cumbric*
caer, a fort, *Gaelic* **càrn** a cairn, or **ceathramh** a
fourth part, or **cathair** a town, a fort, or **càrr** a rock
ledge.

carse *Scots* = a stretch of low-lying land along a river.

clash, cleish from *Gaelic* **clais** a furrow, groove, ditch.

cleugh [klyooch] *Scots* = a gorge, ravine.

coll, collie, colly, killie from *Gaelic* **coille** a wood.

cool see **coul.**

corrie *Scots* spelling of *Gaelic* **coire** a hollow in
mountains, especially one near the top of a hill.

cors(c) frequent *Scots* spelling variant(s) of 'cross'.

coul, cool from *Gaelic* **cùl** the back.

craig, craik from *Gaelic* **creag** a rock, or in some cases
from *Cumbric* **carreg**.

cro(e) usually from *Gaelic* **crò** a cattle-fold, or perhaps
from **crodh** cattle.

dal(l), dail, dol, dul from the *Cumbric* word for a river
meadow (in a valley); usually at the beginning of a
name but very occasionally at the end, as in Cromdale;
see **-dal(l)** below.

-dal(l), -dale, -dail from *Old Norse* **dalr**, a valley; always
at the end of a name; see **dal(l)** above.

damph from *Gaelic* **damh** a stag.

darrach, darroch from *Gaelic* **darach** an oak tree.

dauch, dava(ch), doch from *Gaelic* **dabhach** a vat, tub;
an old land measure (based on the amount of grain
etc. the land could yield).

dhu from *Gaelic* **dubh** black.

din from *Celtic*, meaning a fort: either *Cumbric* **din** or *Gaelic* **dùn**.

doch see **dauch**.

dol see **dal**(l).

doon, doun(**e**) often from *Gaelic* **dùn** a fort.

drochit from *Gaelic* **drochaid** a bridge.

drom, drum from *Gaelic* **druim** the back; a ridge.

dul see **dal**(l).

dum, dun from *Gaelic* **dùn** a fort.

eccle(**s**) either from *Gaelic* **eaglais** or *Cumbric* **eglwys** or directly from their origin, *Latin* **ecclesia**, all meaning church.

edin from *Gaelic* **aodann** a face.

enach, enoch from *Gaelic* **aonach** a hill; a ridge; a moor.

ess from *Gaelic* **eas** a waterfall.

-ey, -ay, -a *Old Norse* **ey** an island.

fal(l) often from *Older Scots, Middle English* **faw** variegated, of different colours.

fas often from *Old Gaelic* = a stance, a place to stop (eg for a night).

fauld *Scots* spelling of 'fold'.

fell from *Old Norse* **fell, fjall** a hill, mountain.

ferin from *Gaelic* **fearran** land; an estate, farm.

fern often from *Gaelic* **feàrna** an alder.

fin(**n**) from *Gaelic* **fionn** white, pale-coloured.

firth *Scots* = an estuary; a wide arm of the sea.

forest a **deer forest** (see Scots section).

gair, gare *Gaelic* **geàrr** short.

gart from *Irish* **gart, gort** or *Cumbric* **garth** a field, enclosure, or *Old Norse* **garðr** an enclosure.

garv from *Gaelic* **garbh** rough.

gate *Scots* (*now mainly in street names*) = a street: *Canongate, Eastgate*.

gil(**le**) *Gaelic* **gille** a boy, young man; a servant (usually referring to the servant of a saint).

glac(k) *Gaelic* **glac** a hollow.

glas(s) from *Gaelic* **glas** grey, greenish-grey, green.

glen from *Gaelic* **gleann** a glen.

gour, gower from *Gaelic* **gabhar, gobhar** a goat.

hal(l)y *Scots* form(s) of 'holy'.

haugh [hawch] *Scots* = a meadow.

heugh [hyooch] *Scots* = a cliff, precipice, steep bank.

hop(e) may be from *Old Norse* **hóp** a bay, or, especially in
      southern Scotland, from *Scots* **hope** an upland valley
      (from *Old English* **hop** a piece of enclosed land).

how(e) *Scots* = a hollow, a basin, a piece of low ground.

inch, ins(c)h from *Gaelic* **innis** a meadow; an island.

inner may be *English* **inner** but frequently from *Gaelic*
      inbhir see **inver**.

ins(c)h see **inch**.

inver from *Gaelic* **inbhir** a rivermouth.

ken see **kin**.

ker may be from *Gaelic* **ceathramh** a fourth part
      (see also **car**); or from *Old Norse* **kjarr** brushwood, a
      thicket.

kil from *Gaelic* **cill** a cell, church, or sometimes from
      coille a wood.

killie see **coll**.

kin, ken from *Gaelic* **ceann** the head.

knock, nock from *Gaelic* **cnoc** a hill.

know(e) *Scots* = a knoll, small hill.

kyle(s) from *Gaelic* **caol** or **caolas** a (narrow) strait.

lag *Gaelic* = a hollow. **laggan** = a little hollow.

laid(e), led from *Gaelic* **leathad** a slope, hillside.

lairig *Gaelic* = a mountain pass.

land *Scots* (*in street names, especially in Edinburgh*)
      = a tenement: *Gladstone's Land*.

law *Scots* = a rounded or conical hill.

lax *Old Norse* = a salmon.

leck from *Gaelic* **leac** a flat stone, slab.

led see **laid(e)**.

leitir see **letter(s)**.

les, lis from *Gaelic* **lios** a garden; an enclosure.

letter(s) from *Gaelic* **leitir** a steep hill slope (often above water).

links see Scots section.

lin(n) from *Gaelic* **linne** a pool or Old English *hlynh* a waterfall, torrent.

lis see **les**.

loan *Scots* = a grassy track, especially a cattle track leading to a pasture; sometimes from *Gaelic* **lòn**.

lon(e), **loan** often from *Gaelic* **lòn** a meadow; a marsh – but see also above.

lui from *Gaelic* **laoigh** of the calf.

lu(i)b from *Gaelic* **lùb** a bend.

machar see **machair** in Gaelic section.

maddy see *Gaelic* **madadh**.

mains *Scots* = the home farm of an estate (*common in farm names*).

màm *Gaelic* = a large rounded hill.

march *Scots* = a boundary.

mell(an), **mell(on)** from *Gaelic* **meall** a rounded hill; **an, on** from *Gaelic* **an** meaning 'of the', or the diminutive ending **-an.**

merse *Scots* = flat land along a river or estuary.

miln- *Older Scots* spelling of 'mill'.

mon(i) usually *Gaelic* **monadh** a hill, moor.

mont, mount may be *English* 'mount' but more frequently *Gaelic* **monadh**.

mo(u)nth from *Gaelic* **monadh**.

more from *Gaelic* **mòr** big.

moss *Scots* = (a stretch of) moorland, boggy ground.

muck often from *Gaelic* **muc** a pig.

mull from *Old Norse* **múli** a headland, but the island of Mull is from an old Gaelic root.

nes(**s**) *Scots* (from *Old English* or *Old Norse*)
= a headland; in Shetland, Orkney and the North-West directly from *Old Norse*; the River Ness however is an ancient river name.

nether as in *English* lower, usually referring to the lower of two places, especially farms.

-nis(**h**) in *Gaelic* **nis**, from *Old Norse* **nes** – see **nes**(**s**) above.

nock see **knock**.

nor *Scots* = north.

òb *Gaelic* = a bay (from *Old Norse* **hóp**).

ochter see **auchter**.

ord *Gaelic* = a hammer.

-our from *Gaelic* **odhar** dun-coloured, fawnish-brown.

pen *Cumbric* the head.

pend (*in street names*) see Scots section.

penny, **pin** from **pennyland**, an old Scots measure of land.

pit, **pet**(**t**) from *Pictish* meaning a share, portion, a farm.

pol(**l**) from *Gaelic* **poll** a pool; a hole; a muddy field; or from *Old Norse* **bólstaðr** – see **-bost**.

-pool see **-bost**.

pres(**s**) from *Gaelic* **preas** a bush; a thicket.

quarrel *Scots* = a quarry.

rannoch, **rannich** from *Gaelic* **raineach** fern; bracken.

ree from *Gaelic* **rìgh** a king, or from **ruighe** a **shieling**, or from **frìth** a **deer forest** (see Scots section).

rhu from *Gaelic* **rubha** a headland, promontory.

rig(**g**) *Scots* = a ridge; in farming, a raised strip of ploughed land between furrows.

ros(**s**) from *Gaelic* **ros** a promontory; or may be from *Old Norse* **hross** a horse.

roy from *Gaelic* **ruadh** red, brownish-red, red-brown.

sauchie [**saw**chee] *Scots* = full of, surrounded by willows.

scaur *Scots* = a steep rock, cliff or bare hill.

-set(t), -setter, -ster, -shader from *Old Norse* **setr** a house, dwelling; may also be from the closely-related *Old Norse* **saetr** a pasture, a **shieling** (see Scots section).

sgor(r), sgurr *Gaelic* = a sharp, steep rock or hill.

shee from *Gaelic* **sìth** peace or **sìthiche** a fairy.

shen from *Gaelic* **sean** old.

sker(ry) from *Old Norse* **sker** a rock in the sea (in *Gaelic* **sgeir**).

slack from *Old Norse* **slakki** a hollow, a valley between hills; some names may be from *Gaelic* **sloc** – see **sloc(k)** below.

slew (*only found in south-west Scotland*) from *Gaelic* **sliabh** a mountain, hill(side), moor.

sloc(k) from *Gaelic* **sloc(hd)** a pit, hollow.

spit(t)al(l), also **spidal, spittle** *Older Scots* = a shelter for travellers, especially in mountains.

-sta from *Old Norse* **staðr** a dwelling, a farm.

stan(e) *Scots* = a stone.

-ster see **-set(t)**.

stob *Gaelic* = a stake, pointed stick; a pointed hill.

strath from *Gaelic* **srath** a broad valley.

stron(e) often from *Gaelic* **sròn** a nose; a point of land.

stuc(k) from *Gaelic* **stuc(hd)** a small jutting hill; a peak; a cliff.

tannach, tannoch from *Old Gaelic* **tamhnach** a green and fertile field.

tar *Gaelic* = across, over.

tarbe(r)t, tarbat from *Gaelic* **tairbeart** an isthmus (literally 'across-bringing').

tarf(f), tarv from *Gaelic* **tarbh** a bull.

tay, tee, ty often from *Gaelic* **taigh** a house; the River Tay however is an ancient *Celtic* river name, meaning 'the silent one'.

temple often name of what was at one time the property of the Knights Templar.

tibber see **tober**.

tillie, tullie, tullich, tulloch from *Gaelic* **tulach** a (smallish) hill.

tipper see **tober**.

tir(e), tyre from *Gaelic* **tìr** land.

tober, tibber, tipper from *Gaelic* **tobar** a well.

tod *Scots* = a fox.

tol(l) s from *Gaelic* **toll** a hole, hollow.

tom *Gaelic* = a small rounded hill.

-ton, -toun from *Old English* **tun** a farm.

tor(r), tore from *Gaelic* **tòrr** a steep conical hill.

-toul from *Gaelic* (**an**) **t-sabhail** of the barn.

tullie, tullich, tulloch see **tillie**.

ty see **tay**.

tyre see **tir(e)**.

-vaig see **-vik**.

-val from *Old Norse* **fjall** a hill, mountain.

vane from *Gaelic* **bhàn**, feminine etc of **bàn** fair.

vat from *Old Norse* **vatn** water, a lake.

vennel *Scots* (*now mainly in street names*) = a narrow street between houses.

-vi(k), -vaig, -vig from *Old Norse* **vík** a bay.

-way, -wall from *Old Norse* **vágr** a bay.

weem *Scots* = a cave (from *Gaelic* **uamh**).

-wick, may be from *Old Norse* **vík** a bay or, in southern Scotland, from *Old English* **wic** a farm.

wynd *Scots* (*now mainly used in street names*) = a narrow street or lane off a main street.

yett *Scots* = a gate; a pass between hills.

SOME SCOTTISH FIRST NAMES
(including familiar forms)

Aeneas see **Angus**.

Agnes from Greek (via Latin) meaning pure, until recently
a very popular girl's name in Scotland. Often shortened
to **Aggie** or **Nessie**. **Senga** is the same name spelt
backwards.

Aileen popular form of Eileen in Scotland; both are of Irish
origin.

Ailie see **Eilidh.**

Ailsa girl's name, probably from Ailsa Craig, a rocky island
in the Firth of Clyde.

Alastair [alastər] Gaelic form of Alexander; also **Alasdair.**
Anglicized spellings include **Alistair, Alister**.

Alison a diminutive form of Alice.

Angus from Gaelic **Aonghas** [oe:nəs], from an old name
probably meaning 'one' + 'choice', sometimes
anglicized as **Aeneas**; shortened to **Gus**.

Bella see **Isabella.**

Beth Scots form of Elizabeth.

Bruce see surname list.

Cailean see **Colin.**

Calum see **Malcolm.**

Cameron see surname list.

Campbell see surname list.

Catriona [kətreeənə] Gaelic form of Catherine.
Sometimes anglicized as **Katrina**.

Coinneach see **Kenneth**.

Colin, a familiar form of Nicholas, it is used as an
anglicised form of Gaelic **Cailean.**

Craig see surname list.

Deirdre name of a heroine of Irish legend who came to
Scotland to escape a family quarrel.

Diarmid [**der**mid] name of a hero of Celtic legend, said to be the progenitor of Clan Campbell.

Donald from Gaelic **Dòmhnall** of Celtic origin, meaning 'world strength'. Shortened to **Don** or **Donnie**.

Dougal, Dugald [**doo**gəl(d)] from Gaelic **Dùghall** from an old name meaning 'black stranger', often shortened to **Doug**(ie) [**doog**(ee)] although, especially in the Lowlands, the latter is more commonly a familiar form of **Douglas**, which is often used as a first name (see surname list); usually pronounced [**dug**(ee)].

Duncan a common Highland name, from Gaelic **Donnchadh**, from an old name meaning 'brown warrior'.

Eachann see **Hector.**

Effie Scots form of Euphemia.

Eilidh [**aylee**] Gaelic form of Helen. Anglicised as **Ailie.**

Ella see **Isabella**.

Elspeth Scots form of Elizabeth.

Ewan, Ewen from Gaelic **Eoghann** of obscure origin.

Farquhar [**far**chər] from Gaelic **Fearchar**, from an old name meaning 'dear man'.

Fergus from Gaelic **Fearghas**, from an old name meaning 'man' + 'strength, bravery'.

Finlay from Gaelic **Fionnlagh**, from an old name meaning 'fair hero'.

Fiona a girl's name invented by the 19th-century writer William Sharp for his pseudonym, Fiona Macleod.

Flora in Latin, a flower goddess, often used as substitute for Gaelic **Fionnghal** meaning 'fair-shouldered'.

Gavin a name of Welsh origin, in Middle English Gawain, it has been popular in Scotland since the Middle Ages.

Geordie Scots form of George.

Gordon see surname list.

Graham see surname list.

Grant see surname list.

Gus see **Angus**.

Hamish from Gaelic **Seumas** James. This name is an anglicized spelling of the vocative case, **a Sheumais** [ə haymish].

Hector used as a substitute for Gaelic **Eachann**, probably meaning 'horseman'.

Hugh used as a substitute for Gaelic names such as **Uisdean**, **Aodh**.

Iain, Ian [eeən] Gaelic form of John.

Iona girl's name from the west-coast island.

Isabella (from the same Hebrew origin as Elizabeth) has long been popular in Scotland in one form or another. **Isobel** is a distinctively Scottish form. Gaelic form is **Iseabail** [eeshəpəl], often anglicized as **Ishbel**. Familiar forms include **Bella**, **Ella**, **Isa**.

Isla girl's name from west-coast island of Islay, or from the river name.

Jamie *Scots* form of James.

Janet has long been popular in Scotland along with familiar forms such as **Jennie** (elsewhere for Jennifer), **Jessie**, and the French-influenced forms **Jeannette**, **Janette** [jənet]. Gaelic form is **Seònaid** [shawnatʸ], sometimes anglicized as **Shona**.

Jean is a popular name, along with its familiar form **Jeanie**. See **Sheena**.

Jock Scots form of John.

Katrina see **Catriona**.

Kenneth from an old Gaelic name **Cined**, but also used as anglicization of Gaelic **Coinneach** [kinyach], from an old name meaning 'fair one'. Shortened to **Ken** or **Kenny**.

Leslie (usually a boy's name), **Lesley** (girl's name) from the surname.

Lindsay a boy's or girl's name, from the surname.

Lorna a name invented by R D Blackmore for the heroine

of his novel *Lorna Doone*. Popular in Scotland probably by association with the place-name **Lorn(e)**, the district in Argyll, which is also used as a first name, mainly but not exclusively for boys.

Mairi [**ma**:ree] Gaelic form of Mary; sometimes spelt **Mhairi** [**va**:ree], the vocative case in Gaelic.

Malcolm from Gaelic **Maol Chaluim** (tonsured) servant of Columba; **Calum** is a Gaelic form.

Marsali Gaelic form of Marjorie.

Mhairi see **Mairi**.

Morag [**moa**:rag], Gaelic **Mòrag** [**moa**:rak], diminutive of **Mòr** meaning 'large, great'; sometimes anglicised as **Marion**.

Murdo, Murdoch from Gaelic **Murchadh**, from an old name meaning 'sea battle'. The first form is a very common first name in the Highlands and the second is also a surname.

Nessie see **Agnes**.

Rab(bie), Rob(bie) Scots forms of Robert.

Raghnall, Ranald see **Ronald**.

Rhona, Rona popular girl's name, perhaps connected with the two islands off the west coast.

Roderick a Germanic name often used as a substitute for Gaelic **Ruaraidh**. Often shortened to **Rod(die)**. See also **Rory**.

Ronald, Ranald in Scotland, probably from the Norse Rögnvald, meaning 'counsel' + 'ruler'. In Gaelic **Raghnall**.

Rory from Gaelic **Ruaraidh** (pronounced **rooə**ree), meaning 'red one'; sometimes spelt **Ruari** but this violates Gaelic spelling rules.

Roy from Gaelic Ruadh 'red-haired'; originally used mainly as a second name, as in Rob **Roy** MacGregor.

Ruaraidh, Ruari see **Rory**.

Senga see **Agnes**.

Seònaid see **Janet**.

Seumas see **Hamish**.

Sheena from Gaelic **Sìne** (pronounced **shee**:nə], Gaelic
form or Jean, Jane.

Sheila from Irish **Síle**, form of Celia, Cecilia. In Scottish
Gaelic **Sìlis** [**shee**:lis].

Shona see **Janet**.

Sìne see **Sheena**.

Tammas, Tam(mie) Scots forms of Thomas.

Uisdean see **Hugh**.

Una [**oo**nə or **yoo**nə] an old Irish name, sometimes
substituted by Winifred or Agnes.

Wilma Scots form of Williamina.

SOME SCOTTISH SURNAMES

The number of Scottish surnames beginning with **Mac** or its contracted forms, **Mc** or **M'** is striking. These are of Gaelic origin, *mac* meaning 'son of'. In English they are used for both sexes but in Gaelic only for males, the female equivalent being **Nic**, 'daughter of'. Thus:

Seumas Mac Coinnich	James MacKenzie
Anna Nic Coinnich	Anne MacKenzie

Some of the *Mac-* names commonly found in Scotland today in fact came over from Ireland in comparatively recent times, especially with the waves of Irish immigrants who came to the industrial Lowlands in the 19th and early 20th centuries. Examples of these are *McGhee* and *McLaughlin* (the usual Scottish spelling being *MacLachlan*).

The contracted forms *Mc* and *M'* are found more frequently with Irish names, though both are also used with Scottish. *M'* is however much less common than it was a generation or two ago.

For those spelt *Mac-* there is the further problem of whether the second part should have a capital letter or not. There is wide disagreement on this point, even among Gaelic speakers. One argument is that a personal name should have a capital but not, for example, a trade name: thus *MacDonald*, but *Macintyre*. Another is that since these names are in anglicized forms, there should be no capital letter in the middle of a word. The first of these has been applied in this list, but practice remains highly variable.

Quite a large number of Scottish surnames are of Norman-French origin, such as *Bruce, Cumming* (or *Comyn*), *Grant, Hay, Sinclair*. They are descended from Anglo-Norman nobles who were given land by the medieval kings of Scots.

Armstrong a Border family, known for their aggressive exploits during the troubled Middle Ages.

Baxter Older Scots for baker.

Bruce a family of Norman-French origin, the name 'de Brus' (from Brix in Normandy) altering to become 'the Bruce' in the name of Scotland's most illustrious medieval king, Robert the Bruce.

Buchanan [bəkanən] from the family's lands on the shores of Loch Lomond.

Cameron from Gaelic **Camshron** 'twisted nose'.

Campbell from Gaelic **Caimbeul** 'twisted mouth'.

Carnegie from the lands in Angus once owned by the family.

Chisholm [tshizəm] from the lands they once owned in Roxburghshire. Some of the family moved to the North in the 14th century, and became a Highland clan.

Colquhoun [kəhoon] from the family's lands on the shores of Loch Lomond.

Craig from Gaelic **creag** a rock.

Cumming or **Comyn** [kumin] a Norman-French name from the plant cumin. The Comyns were powerful landowners in medieval Scotland, rivalling Robert the Bruce in the early 13th century.

Cunningham from the area in the north of Ayrshire where they owned lands.

Dalziel, Dalyell [deeel] from the district of that name in Lanarkshire.

Douglas from the river-name, meaning 'black stream'. The Douglases were one of the most powerful families in medieval Scotland.

Drummond from Drymen near Loch Lomond, although the family lands were later further east in Perthshire.

Forbes [formerly pronounced **for**bis, now usually forbz] from the lands in the valley of the Don in Aberdeenshire.

Fraser or **Frazer** a Norman-French name; their ancestor came to Scotland in the 12th century.

Gilchrist [**gil**krist] from Gaelic **Gille-Crìosd** 'servant of Christ'.

Gillespie [**gile**spee] from Gaelic **Gill-easbuig** 'bishop's servant'.

Gillies [**gi**lis] from Gaelic **Gille Iosa** 'servant of Jesus'.

Gordon from the lands in Berwickshire which the family originally held; they were later granted territory in the North-East by Robert the Bruce.

Gow from Gaelic **gobha** 'a smith'.

Graham their ancestor was an Anglo-Norman noble, the name of whose English manor meant grey home.

Grant a Norman-French name from French 'le Grand' the big one.

Hay a Norman-French name from La Haye in Normandy.

Innes from the coastal area in Moray.

Leslie from the area in Aberdeenshire.

Lindsay an Anglo-Norman family, the name coming from Lindsey, probably meaning 'island of the lime tree', in Northern England.

MacBeth from Gaelic **Mac Bheatha** 'son of life.

MacInnes from Gaelic **Mac Aonghuis** 'son of Angus'.

Macintyre from Gaelic **Mac an t-saoir** 'son of the carpenter'.

MacKay from Gaelic **Mac Aoidh** 'son of **Aodh'**, an old Gaelic name, sometimes anglicized as Hugh.

MacKenzie from Gaelic **Mac Coinnich** 'son of **Coinneach'**, an old Gaelic name anglicized as **Kenneth**. Formerly pronounced [mə**king**ee] – for the 'z' in spelling, see Introduction.

MacKinnon from Gaelic **Mac Fhionghain,** 'son of Fingan' (an old Gaelic name meaning 'fair-born').

Mackintosh from Gaelic **Mac an Tòisich**, 'son of the toiseach or chief'.

MacLaren, MacLaurin from Gaelic **Mac Labhruinn** 'son of Laurence'.

Maclean [məklayn] from Gaelic **Mac Gill-Eathain** 'son of the servant of John'.

MacLeod [məklowd] from Gaelic **Mac Leòid** 'son of Leod', a 13th-century Norse ancestor (Norse **Ljótr** 'ugly').

Macpherson from Gaelic **Mac a' Phearsoin** 'son of the parson'.

Mactaggart from Gaelic **Mac an t-Sagairt** 'son of the priest'.

MacTavish from Gaelic **Mac Thàmhais** 'son of Tammas', Scots form of Thomas.

Menzies a Norman-French name (from Mesnières in Normandy), now often pronounced as it is spelt, but Scottish pronunciation is [**ming**is] or [**meeng**is] – for the 'z' in spelling, see Introduction.

Mor(r)ison son of Morris, but used in the Highlands and Islands as an anglicization of Gaelic, either **Mac Ghille Mhoire**, 'son of the servant of Mary', or
O Muirgheasàin, name of an Irish family who became hereditary poets to Scottish clan chiefs. In modern Gaelic, **Moireasdan**.

Murray from Moray in North-East Scotland.

Ogg from Gaelic **òg** young.

Ogilvie from the lands in Angus.

Ross from the former northern county.

Sinclair [**sing**klər] a Norman-French name from Saint-Clair-sur-Elle in Normandy.

Stewart ancestors of some Stewarts were hereditary Stewards of Scotland, an important office at the medieval Scottish court. Through the marriage of Walter the Steward to Marjorie, daughter of King Robert the Bruce, Scotland, and later Great Britain, acquired a line of Stewart monarchs. The spelling **Stuart**, latterly used by the royal house, is due to French influence, probably at the time of Mary, Queen of Scots.

Sutherland from the area in the extreme north-west of Scotland (which was nevertheless 'south-land' to the Norsemen).

Urqhuart [**ur**chart] from the place-name in Inverness-shire.

Wallace means Welsh, probably referring to the British inhabitants of Strathclyde, what is now south-west Scotland; see p. 68.

Webster Older Scots for weaver.

FOOD AND DRINK
See also Scots-English and Gaelic-English section.

Scottish food at its wholesome best can be of very high
quality. Some of the natural ingredients produced in this
small and seemingly unfavourable part of the world are
unsurpassed anywhere. The meat, especially hill lamb and
beef, is prized the world over, as is Scottish trout and
salmon, now, thanks to fish farms, more widely available.
Shellfish are also of high quality, including lobsters,
langoustines, crabs, oysters, mussels and scallops. Game
birds abound, especially pheasant and grouse, and Scotland
does not sufficiently appreciate the venison from the large
red-deer population, as a high proportion of it is exported
to Europe.

Certain parts of Scotland produce excellent soft fruits,
especially raspberries and strawberries, in Tayside and
other areas. Wild raspberries are one of the pleasures of
the countryside, as are blaeberries (small blue berries) on
the hills and moors, and blackberries in the autumn
(known here as brambles),

Perhaps the food most associated with Scotland is oats,
and its food value, one of the main reasons for the good
health of Scots in the past, is now much more widely
appreciated. Everyone has heard of porridge, oatcakes and
haggis, but there are numerous other dishes of which it is
the main ingredient; the following is a small selection of
these:

Athole brose a mixture of oatmeal, honey, whisky and
water.
bannock a round flat cake, usually made of oatmeal, but
thicker and softer than an oatcake.
brose oatmeal mixed with boiling water or milk, with salt,

butter etc added. Special varieties are also eaten,
especially in the North-East, such as **neep brose**, made
with water in which turnips have been cooked. Once the
staple diet of country folk.

crannachan a dessert of whipped cream, toasted oatmeal,
berries etc, based on a Highland harvest dish.

mealie pudding a kind of sausage made of oatmeal, suet,
onions, seasoning.

skirlie similar ingredients fried.

Scots housewives have long been known for their skill in
baking and a large variety of cakes and other baking can
also be found in shops throughout the country. The names
of some of these examples have to be distinguished from
their English or American counterparts.

sweet

black bun or **Scotch bun** a very rich spicy fruit cake,
baked in a pastry case, eaten at New Year.

cookie a round, light, sweet, dark-glazed bun, made with a
yeast dough; sometimes filled with whipped cream
(**cream cookie**).

Dundee cake a rich fruit cake with almonds on top.

Selkirk bannock a large round yeasted bun with sultanas.

shortbread a kind of crisp crumbly biscuit made of flour,
butter and sugar, traditional fare at New Year.

less sweet

Abernethy biscuit a kind of large, light crisp biscuit.

crumpet a very thin largish **pancake** (see below), often
rolled up with jam etc inside.

pancake or **dropped scone** a small round flat cake baked
by dropping a very soft dough onto a **girdle** etc.

parkin a kind of spiced biscuit made of oatmeal, flour,
treacle etc.

potato scone or **tattie scone** a thin flat cake made of mashed potatoes, flour, butter and salt.

soda scone a scone made of a soft dough of plain flour, bicarbonate of soda, cream of tartar and buttermilk, baked on a **girdle** etc, usually in a large round cut into triangular sections.

There is also a great variety of sweets, or sweeties, such as:

black man a kind of dark-coloured candy or toffee, made with treacle.

black strippit ba(ll) a hard, round, peppermint-flavoured sweet with black and white stripes.

boiling a boiled sweet.

cheugh Jeans or **teuch Jeans** [tshuch] a kind of very chewy toffee.

Edinburgh rock a light, stick-shaped sweet made of sugar, water and cream of tartar, with flavouring and pastel colouring.

Hawick ba(ll) a hard round cinnamon or mint-flavoured sweet, made in Hawick.

Jeddart snail a kind of dark toffee, made in Jedburgh.

oddfellow a small pastel-coloured sweet, flavoured with cinnamon etc.

pan drop a round white peppermint sweet, a mint imperial.

soor ploom a tart-flavoured round green boiled sweet.

tablet a kind of fudge, of a hard consistency.

Scotland's national drink is usually considered to be whisky, although its history as a prestige drink does not go as far back as one might imagine. The favoured drink of the upper classes in the past was claret and the wine trade between Edinburgh (or rather Leith) and Bordeaux from the early Middle Ages has been well documented. Today however whisky is one of our most popular drinks, and one of our chief exports.

Whisky is sometimes known as barley bree, but the name
is appropriate only to one of the two types of whisky
produced – **malt whisky**, which is distilled from malted
barley only. This is the more refined drink and is produced
by a very large number of manufacturers whose resounding
names – Glenlivet, Glenfiddich, Glenmorangie – may be
seen in profusion around the shelves of many bars. The
more ordinary drink is **blended whisky**, made from a
mixture of malt whisky and whisky made from grain
(usually maize). Some blends are given additional flavour,
prestige – and price – by a higher proportion of malt to
grain.

Beer is also drunk in large quantities in Scotland and its
terminology differs from that south of the Border:

heavy: approximately as English bitter.
export or **80/-**: a slightly stronger and darker-coloured
beer than heavy.
light: a low-gravity beer which may be dark in colour.
IPA or **pale ale**: a medium-gravity beer, often light in
colour, cream or smoothflow: similar to heavy but less
carbonated.

The real ale movement has had some success in Scotland
and has led to the re-introduction of small craft breweries
in many parts of the country. Some produce specialist beers
using Scottish ingredients such as heather or berries and
many have local (including Scots and Gaelic) names.

FURTHER INFORMATION

SCOTS LANGUAGE
Dictionaries
Concise Scots Dictionary 1985, 862 pp, a comprehensive one-volume dictionary covering the Scots language from its earliest records to the present, based largely on the two major historical works:

Scottish National Dictionary 1931-76, 10 vols, from 1700
 to the 1970s, and:
Dictionary of the Older Scottish Tongue 1931-2002, 12 vols,
 from the earliest records up to 1700.
 Both of these are now available free on the Internet, as
 the *Dictionary of the Scots Language,* at www.dsl.ac.uk.
 A New Supplement bringing the language into the
 21st century was added in 2005.
Pocket Scots Dictionary 1988, 684 pp, Scots-English.
Concise English-Scots Dictionary 1993, 319 pp.
Essential Scots Dictionary (Scots-English, English-Scots)
 1996, 382 pp.
Collins Scots Dictionary 2003, 286 pp.

General
For general information and history of Scots, see also the introductions to the above dictionaries.

David Murison *The Guid Scots Tongue* 1977, 63 pp, an essay
 on Scots and its history.
The New Testament in Scots 1963, a translation from the original
 languages by W L Lorimer.
J Derrick McClure *Why Scots Matters* 2nd edn 1997,
 74 pp.
Charles Jones ed. *The Edinburgh History of the Scots Language*
 1997, 700 pp
John Corbett *Language and Scottish Literature* 1997,
 283 pp.
John Corbett et al eds. *Edinburgh Companion to Scots* 2003,
 317 pp. Essays on various aspects of Scots.

Organisations and websites

Scottish Language Dictionaries:

    27 George Square, Edinburgh EH8 9LD

    tel and fax: 0131 650 4149

    email: mail@scotsdictionaries.org.uk

    website: www.scotsdictionaries.org.uk

Scots Language Resource Centre

    A. K. Bell Library, York Place, Perth PH2 8EP

    tel: 01738 440199, fax: 477010

    email: office@scotsyett.com website: www.scotsyett.com

Association for Scottish Literary Studies:

    c/o Department of Scottish History, University of Glasgow,

    9 University Gardens, Glasgow G12 8QH

    tel: 0141 330 5309, fax: 4576

    email: office@asls.org.uk website: www.asls.org.uk

GAELIC

Dictionaries etc

Edward Dwelly *The Illustrated Gaelic-English Dictionary* 1911, 1034 pp, a remarkably comprehensive dictionary, written by an Englishman at the end of the 19th century; packed with interesting information, but not easy for the learner to use.

Malcolm McLennan *A pronouncing and Etymological Dictionary of the Gaelic Language: Gaelic-English, English-Gaelic* 1925, 613 pp.

Abair faclan! small Gaelic-English-English-Gaelic dictionary 1979, 170 pp.

Derick Thomson *The New English-Gaelic Dictionary* 1981, 210 pp.

Morag MacNeill *Everyday Gaelic* new edn 2006, 144pp.

Robert C Owen *The Modern Gaelic-English Dictionary: Am Faclair Ùr Gàidhlig-Beurla* 1993, 149 pp.

Angus Watson *The Essential Gaelic-English Dictionary: A Dictionary for Students and Learners of Scottish Gaelic* 2001, 434 pp; *The Essential English-Gaelic Dictionary* 2005, 437pp.

Boyd Robertson and Ian Macdonald *Teach Yourself Gaelic Dictionary* Gaelic-English 2004, 332 pp.

Colin Mark *The Gaelic-English Dictionary: Am Faclair Gàidhlig-Beurla* 2004, 784 pp.

Courses

Robeard Ó Maolalaigh with Iain MacAoghnuis *Hugo's Scottish Gaelic in Three Months* 1996, 236 pp.

Boyd Robertson and Iain Taylor *Teach Yourself Gaelic: A complete course for beginners* 1993, 344 pp.

Speaking our Language originally from TV programmes (4 series of 18 programmes), available in books, tapes and videos.

Organisations and websites

An Comunn Gàidhealach: 109 Church Street, Inverness
    IV1 1EY tel: 01463 231226, fax: 715557
    email: info@ancomunn.co.uk
    website: www.ancomunn.co.uk
    Organisation founded in 1891 to promote Gaelic; organises a festival of music and poetry, the Royal National Mod.

Association for Scottish Literary Studies see Scots section, above.

Bòrd na Gàidhlig: Darach House, Stoneyfield Business Park, Inverness IV2 7PA tel: 01463 225454, fax: 716217
    email: fios@bord-na-gaidhlig.org.uk
    website: www.bord-na-gaidhlig.org.uk
    Government organisation set up to stimulate and fund Gaelic projects.

Clì Gàidhlig: 3 Union Street, Inverness IV1 1PP
    tel/fax: 01463 226710 email: cli@cli.org.uk
    website: www.cli.org.uk
    Organisation which coordinates learner activities; quarterly bilingual magazine *Cothrom*. It also has a website - www.learn-gaelic.info - with detailed information for learners, on classes, course, clubs etc.

Comunn na Gàidhlig: 5 Mitchells Lane, Inverness IV2 3HQ
    tel: 01463 234138, fax: 237470 email: oifis@cnag.org.uk
    website: www.cnag.org.uk
    Government-funded organisation which helps Gaelic development, especially in education.

Sabhal Mòr Ostaig: Sleat, Isle of Skye IV44 8RQ
    tel: 01471 888000, fax: 888001
    email smo.oifis@smo.uhi.ac.uk
    website: www.smo.uhi.ac.uk
    Gaelic college with courses on Gaelic and in other subjects in Gaelic.

PLACE-NAMES

David Dorward *Scotland's Place-Names* 1995, 171 pp.

Alexander MacBain *Place-names Highlands and Islands of Scotland* 1922, 413 pp.

W F H Nicolaisen *Scottish Place-names* 1976, 2001.
A descriptive study rather than a reference book.

W J Watson *The History of the Celtic Place-names of Scotland* 1926, 578 pp. Still the standard work on an important aspect of Scottish place-names.

For mountain names, *Munro's Tables and other tables of lower hills* 1997 edition, 176 pp, contains an appendix with explanations of the names of Munros and Corbetts, and for more detailed information: Peter Drummond *Scottish Hill and Mountain Names: The origins and meaning of the names of Scotland's hills and mountains* 1991, 224 pp.

Regional studies include:

William Alexander *The Place-names of Aberdeenshire* 1952.

Richard A V Cox *The Gaelic Place-Names of Carloway, Isle of Lewis: their structure and significance* 2002, 496 pp.

Angus Macdonald *The Place-Names of West Lothian* 1941, 190 pp.

Ian A Fraser *The Place-Names of Arran* 1999 168 pp.

Ruaraidh MacIlleathain (Roddy Maclean) *The Gaelic Place Names and Heritage of Inverness* 2005, 96 pp.

Hugh Marwick *Orkney Farm Names* 1952.

Simon Taylor *Place-Names of Fife* (Vol. 1, West Fife between Leven and Forth) 2006, 600+ pp.

Adam Watson and Elizabeth Allan *The Place Names of Upper Deeside* 1984, 220 pp.

W J Watson *Place-names of Ross and Cromarty* 1904, 220 pp.

Organisations and websites

Scottish Place-Name Society (Comann Ainmean-Aite na h-Alba), a voluntary organsation which coordinates the work of different groups and individuals, from academics to interested laymen. Twice-yearly newsletter.
website: www.st-andrews.ac.uk/institutes/sassi/spns.

The Ordnance Survey has a new Internet publication elucidating Gaelic, Welsh, Norse and Scots terms on its maps (replacing its earlier pamphlets): www.ordnancesurvey.co.uk

PERSONAL NAMES

George F Black *The Surnames of Scotland* 1946, 920 pp.

David Dorward *Scottish Surnames* 2002, 384 pp.

Patrick Hanks and Flavia Hodges *A Dictionary of Surnames* 1988, 880 pp.

Patrick Hanks and Flavia Hodges *A Dictionary of First Names* 1990, 489 pp.

Donald Whyte *Scottish Forenames: their origins and history* 1996, 205 pp.

FOOD AND DRINK

Cookery books

Catherine Brown *Scottish Cookery* 1985, 304 pp, interesting book to browse through as well as a recipe book, traditional and modern.

Catherine Brown *A Year in the Scots Kitchen* 1996, 194 pp.

Sue Lawrence *Scots Cookery* 2000, 192 pp. Traditional and modern recipes with interesting notes.

F Marian McNeill *The Scots Kitchen its Traditions and Lore with Old-time Recipes* 1929, 275 pp. A standard work of the early 20th century.

General

Catherine Brown *From Broths to Bannocks* 1990, 273 pp. A history of Scottish food and cooking from the 17th century on.

Geddes, Olive *The Laird's Kitchen: Three hundred years of food in Scotland* 1994, 119 pp.

Steven, Maisie *The Good Scots Diet* new edition 2003, 160 pp.

Drink

Tom Bruce-Gardyne *The Scotch Whisky Book* 2002, 240 pp. Includes a guide to distilleries.

David Daiches *Scotch Whisky Past and Present* 1969, 176 pp.

Neil M Gunn *Whisky and Scotland* 1935, 198 pp. Whisky and its history and the novelist's views on both.

Billy Kay and Cailean Maclean *Knee Deep in Claret* 1983, 232 pp. A history of wine-drinking in Scotland (casting doubt on what is really Scotland's national drink).

F Marian MacNeill *The Scots Cellar: its tradition and lore* 1967, 1973, 301 pp.